THE PORNOGRAPHY PARADOX

WHY LDS MEN ARE TOO OFTEN TRAPPED IN
PORNOGRAPHY AND SEXUAL ADDICTION —
AND HOW TO BREAK FREE

STEPHEN MOORE, LCSW, CSAT
AND MARK KASTLEMAN, BCC, BCPC

THE PORNOGRAPHY PARADOX:
How LDS Men Are Too Often Trapped in Pornography and
Sexual Addiction—And How to Break Free.
Copyright 2018 © by Stephen Moore & Mark Kastleman

All rights reserved. Except as permitted under the U.S. Copyright Act of 1976, no part of this book may be reproduced, distributed, or transmitted in any form or by any means, or stored in a database or retrieval system without the written permission of the authors, except in the case of brief passages embodied in critical reviews and articles where the title, author and ISBN accompany such review or article.

Another quality title from InnerLight Solutions, LLC

Visit us at: www.innerlightsolutionsllc.com

Cover Design and Layout by Francine Eden Platt
Eden Graphics, Inc., www.edengraphics.net

Editor: Carrie Moore, MS

ISBN 978-1-7320745-0-7

Printed in the United States of America

For our wives and their amazing love, patience, and support.

And for every addict and spouse who has been touched by this addiction: may you find help, hope and healing in these pages.

CONTENTS

Introduction vii

Section One: The Problem

1 Our Stories: The Journey from Sexual Addiction to Freedom. 3
2 Beyond the Birds and the Bees: Cultural Confusion About Sex. 19
3 Our Sex-Saturated Society is a Set-Up 23
4 Sexual Shame In A Religious Culture. 27
5 We're Outside Christ's Circle, Trying to Earn Our Way Back In. 31
6 Sexually Obsessed: Sex as a Substitute for Connection With Others 35
7 The Funnel: The Science Behind Why We Act Out Sexually 40
8 Pornography Use is Substance Abuse 45
9 Am I Beyond Saving?. 49
10 Sexual Addiction is Not About Sex! 52
11 Using Sex as a Means to Cope With Trauma 55
12 The Avoidance Cycle: Why Trying Harder Doesn't Work 59
13 How You're Fighting is Part of the Problem. 65
14 "God and I Can Handle This Just Fine" . . . Really? 69
15 The Doctor Will See You Now, But Are You Willing to See Him? 74
16 The More You Drink Salt Water, the More You Thirst. 80
17 Sexual Addiction is an *Intimacy Disorder*. 84

Section Two: The Solution

1 The Role of Acceptance and Willingness in Lasting Recovery............93

2 Receiving God's Unconditional Love and Acceptance................... 98

3 The Gift of Grace: The Power Behind Your Recovery 104

4 Establishing Physical, Emotional and Spiritual Boundaries With Yourself.. 110

5 Connecting In Healthy Ways: Setting Boundaries With Others.......... 115

6 You are NOT Your Brain!.. 119

7 Clearing Away the Wreckage of Your Past..............................124

8 Walking Through Walls: Healing the Core Causes of Addiction..........129

9 Ego-Brain Tendencies vs. Eternal Self Attributes.......................134

10 Holding Yourself Accountable While Accepting Your Humanity 139

11 Stop Doing It Your Way—To Win, You Must Surrender!.................143

12 Recovery Requires Real Connection 150

13 Taking the Fight to the Enemy 157

14 Creating Your Battle Plan for Successful Recovery..................... 161

Additional Resources

For the Spouse of An Addict...169

Can Our Marriage Survive?..173

Help for Priesthood Leaders...177

Contact the Authors 180

About the Authors 181

INTRODUCTION

As counselors specializing in sexual addiction treatment and recovery, we have been blessed with the sacred opportunity of helping individuals and couples from many different faiths, backgrounds and circumstances, here in the U.S. and in various parts of the world. Because we are both Latter-day Saints and our home base is in the state of Utah, it has also been our great privilege to work closely with many of our LDS brothers and sisters.

Something that has caused us great concern, and has been a major part of the passion and impetus behind this book, is the pandemic of secrecy, fear and shame that we see among LDS men hopelessly trapped in pornography and other sexual addiction behaviors. So many desperately want and need help, and yet relatively few are willing to take what they perceive as the frightening risk of full disclosure. Many are *addicts in disguise,* sitting in elders quorums and high priests groups; others have been excommunicated, disfellowshipped, or have left the church. All feel uniquely flawed, weak and wicked. Yet, all around them are men with similar struggles, equally afraid to open up and get the help they need.

We have a special heart-felt empathy and understanding for those of our faith who strain under the heavy burden of pornography and sexual addiction. As young teens, we were exposed to pornography, quickly entrapped, and over time became deeply addicted. As you will learn, pornography addiction is a subset of *sexual addiction,* which encompasses a maze of many behaviors. The sexual addiction path nearly always begins with some form of pornography use. Such was the case for us.

Our journey to becoming counselors in this field was paved with the pain, shame, frustration and exhaustion of our own decades-long battles with sexual addiction. In the midst of our desperate struggles, we continued to be active priesthood holders. Through prescribed priesthood channels and honest, sincere repentance, we enjoyed wonderful periods of sobriety as we served full-time missions and were each married in the temple. Yet always, the addiction would eventually rear its ugly head and the battle would begin again: a cycle of repeatedly repenting and falling back, spanning decades of our lives. Yet through it all we continued yearning and striving to live the Gospel of Jesus Christ; served in callings; exercised our priesthood; provided for and presided over our families. We continually felt like *Dr. Jekyll and Mr. Hyde;* walking contradictions plagued by duplicity and trapped in a shameful *Pornography Paradox*!

The Pornography Paradox

Our greatest desire in writing this book is to reach out to all LDS men who find themselves trapped in the *paradox* that held us bound for so many years. *Paradox* is defined as an *absurd dichotomy, incongruity or contradiction*. For LDS men who find themselves hopelessly shackled in pornography use and other sexual addiction-related behaviors, pornography is the *ultimate paradox!*

Pornography is simultaneously repulsive and alluring—it goes against everything an LDS man holds dear and yet too often he is irresistibly attracted to it. Pornography hijacks the natural, beautiful, divinely designed gift of sexuality and twists it into a dark, destructive tool of the adversary. LDS men trapped in sexual addiction yearn to be followers of Christ, yet find themselves giving in to destructive behaviors that disconnect them from God and their loved ones. Most LDS men deeply desire to honor and protect women. But again and again, they give in to behaviors that bring the women in their lives great pain and betrayal. Younger LDS men long to serve missions and be married in the temple, but continue engaging in sexual behaviors that block these righteous desires. All of these men love the light, and at the same time find themselves repeatedly walking into the darkness.

Yes, pornography and sexual addiction do create a confusing, frustrating and exasperating paradox for LDS men. Yet, as men who have been where you now are, we stand as witnesses to the absolute truth—*you do NOT need to remain a slave to this insidious paradox any longer!* In the pages that follow, we will openly share the details of our own personal journeys out of the prison of sexual addiction, and the successful transformations of men we have helped over the years. If we can do it, you can do it!

Helpful Guidelines as You Read

We have authored this book in an unusual way: each chapter is written by a single author—either Stephen Moore or Mark Kastleman. You will find the name of the author for each chapter directly beneath the chapter title. This unique approach allows us to speak personally to you from our individual experiences as counselors, priesthood holders and sexual addicts in long-term successful recovery.

Throughout the book you will notice examples of *cultural practices* within the church vs. *doctrinal principles*. In our personal experience, and in working with our LDS clients, we have observed various traditions and practices that naturally develop in every ward, stake and area of the church. Some of these *cultural* paradigms can perpetuate the shame and secrecy of sexual addiction.

Our purpose is to let you *see* through the eyes of LDS men struggling with sexual addiction and how they can interpret different aspects of their faith. The *lens of shame* created by sexual addiction greatly twists and distorts many of the beautiful doctrines of the gospel. We invite you now to take the next step on your journey toward lasting peace and freedom.

SECTION ONE
THE PROBLEM

OUR STORIES:
THE JOURNEY FROM SEXUAL ADDICTION TO FREEDOM

MY STORY BY STEPHEN MOORE

I AM A HUSBAND and hope to be a father one day. I am a "temple-worthy" Latter-day Saint and active in my congregation. I am a mental health therapist and the owner of a private counseling practice. I am also in successful recovery from the sexual addiction I have battled for more than 20 years.

I wasn't always so open about my addiction. For much of my life, I was secretive and guarded about sharing any part of my story. Until I began the journey to real recovery, it was always a shameful secret that I carried; one that had to be hidden at all costs from everyone around me. Prior to beginning the journey of lasting recovery, I would rather have died than let anyone find out. I was naive, lacked knowledge, and progressively fell into denial about the impact and scope of my addiction. For much of my life, I was not even fully aware of the significance of what I was struggling with.

The Stage is Set

At the age of 12, my life seemed to be moving in a good direction. I was enrolled in junior high and was slowly developing more friendships. I was a couple of years into the process of settling into the "normal routine" of a typical kid, having been in remission for just over a year following two separate battles with a rare form of leukemia. I had spent a good portion of my childhood up to that point in the hospital. Cancer is serious business, and I found myself growing up in many respects at a very young age. After achieving remission, I found it difficult to relate to other kids my age; we saw the world very differently. Needless to say, it was nice to be focusing less on staying alive, and more on friends, cartoons, and other carefree "kid stuff." The normalcy was short-lived. Less than 18 months after my bone-marrow transplant, my Dad was killed in a plane crash, and everything in my world changed.

My best friend. My hero. My Dad. Gone in an instant. Over the course of the following weeks and months, what began as grief turned into anger, which slowly turned toxic. I was angry at God for taking my Dad away after allowing me to struggle with cancer twice. Angry at my Mom, because I couldn't be angry at my Dad, and she was the next closest thing—an easy target. Angry at the world, because the people who played a role in my father's plane crash were killed in that same accident and couldn't be held accountable. Angry at myself, carrying a distorted notion of "survivor's guilt:" I should have known something like this was coming, and I should have stopped it.

Emotionally, I isolated from my sisters and mother for various reasons. I decided that maintaining emotional distance was best, 1) because I now had to be their "protector," which meant not showing emotion or weakness, and 2) the thought of getting close to someone else made me nervous for fear of being hurt again. My uncle, who became my father figure following my Dad's death, also died suddenly less than four years later. At this point I learned a dangerous and distorted paradigm: when I get close to others, be it God or people, they abandon me; they go away; they hurt me. Why get close to anyone, only to have them go away?

I had all these feelings inside, but no one I felt safe to share them with. Emotionally, I felt entirely alone in a room full of people. I wanted to believe that God loved me and would listen, but struggled to see how He was doing so. Between the cancer, the loss of my Dad, and the loss of my uncle, I couldn't see how God loved me, much less cared about my happiness. I was convinced that no one could understand what I was feeling.

Unplugging from the Spiritual

I believed in God and was raised to believe that being obedient brought blessings. But I was feeling shortchanged in the "blessings" category. I began to believe I'd done something horrible, sufficient to warrant the "punishment" I was experiencing. If God loved me, I thought, why would He let this all happen? So I bottled up these feelings, wrapped them in a bundle of resentment, shame and trauma, and shoved it all down into the darkest corners of myself. Little did I know this would become a pattern that would continue long into the future. The emotional and spiritual isolation I felt was coupled with my unresolved anger, grief and shame. My thinking became dangerously skewed. The "perfect storm" for addiction was brewing.

Finding My "Escape"

About this time, I discovered the department store ads for women's underwear that came in the Sunday newspaper. To an emotionally healthy and secure person, these would be considered just that: ads for underwear. But for a 12-year-old with raging hormones and unresolved anger, they were instantly alluring. Emotionally isolated and desperate for an escape, I felt like God and everyone I cared about had abandoned me. It was the ultimate setup: a combination of emotional trauma, toxic feelings, social isolation, and sexual curiosity. The ads fostered a fantasy where my problems didn't matter. This pornography (yes, these advertisements were pornographic to me; more on this later) made me feel good in ways that I never had. It allowed me to escape the depression and anger that was raging inside me. I had found a way to cope. A terribly destructive one, as I would come to find out, but a way to cope, nonetheless. While these images helped me escape for only a short time, when lost in them, I didn't have to face the emotions I was running from. For me, it was the emotional equivalent of finding an oasis while alone in the desert. Pornography became my heroin, my cocaine, my alcohol: my drug.

Not long after this I discovered masturbation. A full sexual release was even more intoxicating than the pornography alone had been. I also began seeking what most consider to be more "hardcore" pornography. I quickly found I could use both the pornography and masturbation not just as an escape from my feelings, but to cope with difficult situations and emotions as they arose. Not accepted by others at school? Girls not paying attention to me? Feeling inadequate in nearly every area of life? No problem; the actors in my fantasy world were always willing to accept me, with no strings attached. The images would instantly transport me to a place where sex is the ultimate form of acceptance. A place where love and value is measured by the lengths to which the actors in these pictures and films will go. In my fantasy world, their willingness to be sexual with me was a measure of my worth as a person.

Going Down the Rabbit Hole

As I continued acting out, sex was becoming ingrained in me as the ultimate hallmark for acceptance—the *only* form of genuine human connection. Each time I would act out to escape shame and guilt, the shallow connection and pleasure I felt was always short-lived. Even worse, it was immediately followed by more shame and guilt. My emotional isolation deepened, and a warped sense of connection grew. My naivety and denial about the nature of my problem numbed me to the bigger picture. Like a child playing with matches who is oblivious to the gunpowder keg he's sitting on, I was on a terribly destructive and dangerous path. Yet, I convinced myself that I was simply dealing with "a little porn problem."

What I now recognize as an addiction grew, becoming progressively compulsive and destructive, both in frequency and in types of behavior. I would have periods of abstinence, sometimes as long as several months, then convince myself that I was done with these behaviors: that I was cured. But despite my best intentions, I wasn't able to permanently put it down. I was hooked. The more I engaged in my addiction, the more I became dependent on it. I met with LDS priesthood leader after priesthood leader seeking help. They did their best to assist, but had little training or knowledge about sexual addiction. After each meeting, I would try to do what they said in order to free myself from my addiction, only to struggle and relapse again. The longer this cycle repeated itself, the more hopeless and desperate I became. I wondered whether I would ever be able to stop. As I began to lose hope of any lasting recovery, figuring out how to simply act out less became my goal. At the same time, I was incredibly naïve about the significance of what I was involved in. I desperately wanted to stop, but didn't know how to cope without my drug. While harmful, it was "normal" to me at the time. I came to believe that everyone struggled with pornography to one degree or another. This pattern continued through high school and during my preparation to serve an LDS mission.

"Cured?"

In many ways, I had a lot going for me. Those observing my outward behaviors considered me to be "on the right track." I spent my senior year serving on my high school's LDS Seminary Council. I was voted by my peers in the yearbook as "most likely to become a seminary teacher." As a young man, I had always wanted to serve a mission. I would fill with pride just thinking of the chance to go out there and serve; to teach others about the gospel, and to touch lives through service. My mission would be my chance to somehow "make up" for the poor choices in my past. The future looked bright, and I resolved to tackle my addiction as never before.

Eventually, I put enough "sobriety" time together to serve a mission. I had a wonderful and fruitful mission largely free of sexual obsession or acting out. I worked hard, and was blessed to play a role in helping many people. "This is it," I thought. "I'm cured." I didn't have to look at myself as a terrible person anymore—I was "normal." My acting out was comparatively non-existent and I concluded that the problem had been eradicated. I was wrong.

I returned home after successfully completing my mission and began going out with an amazing woman I had briefly dated in high school. We fell in love, and after a lot of prayer and discussion we got engaged. It is an understatement to say that I married the girl of my dreams. Early in our courtship, I was open with my future wife about my past, though looking back, both of us were naive about the significance and deep-rooted nature of my addiction. I had equated sobriety with being "healed." But I wasn't. Neither of us had any concept of the danger we were walking into.

The True Nature of Addiction

For the first year and a half of our marriage, I remained free from acting out. We were happy; life was blissful. We were active in our church callings and I was serving in a bishopric. The days of sexual compulsion felt like a distant memory. I had never imagined that marriage could be so amazing. But slowly, the addiction's pull began to creep back in. They were small slips at first – too long gazing at something pornographic that accidentally came up while online; too little caution about what websites I was visiting. This quickly spiraled to actively acting out in my addiction once again.

I immediately told my wife. She was surprised, but remained encouraging and supportive; we were hopeful that we could beat this thing together. However, we lacked a full understanding of what we were dealing with, or any knowledge about how to recover. I quickly fell into the same pattern of talking to priesthood leaders and getting some "white knuckled" sobriety time, only to repeatedly relapse. This cycle caused further damage, hurting my sweet wife and harming our marriage over and over again.

As years passed, my poor choices and behaviors began to take a toll on our relationship. My acting out and betrayal—coupled with my emotional reactivity as I tried to live without my "drug"—was driving both my wife and my marriage away. I was too caught up in shame, pride and pain to see it at the time, but I was risking everything that was important to me.

Real Change Begins

When we finally realized the significance of the issue (not an overnight process, to be sure), I gradually got more serious about finding real recovery. I was introduced to the concept of "sexual addiction" and what it meant through miraculous and providential events, facilitated by a Heavenly Father who still loved me despite my belief to the contrary. I shifted my educational focus to the field of mental health, in part to figure myself out. I was guided to jobs working with one addiction or another. Each of them helped me to gradually chip through the denial and naivety that had plagued me for nearly 20 years. I eventually began therapy and started attending support groups. I began working the 12 Steps of addiction recovery, and my wife and I began working on our marriage with the assistance of a therapist.

"A Whole New Way of Life"

After years of work, tears, heartache, and countless resources invested in recovery, the emotional and marital destruction that my addiction left in its wake is now mending. We still have many obstacles to overcome, both individually and as a couple. Through the grace of God and the support of those closest to me (most significantly my patient wife), *I have been free from sexual compulsion* and acting out for years now. A lot of healing is still needed, but I'm grateful to say that we're in the best place we've been in years, and have real hope for our future. We're on an exciting journey of rediscovering the peace and joy that a life free of addiction can bring. We're growing and learning, both individually and as a couple.

Now in a real place of recovery, I am happier and more connected with God and others than I have ever been. Instead of hiding my past, I have come to accept it. Though difficult, I've decided to share my story with anyone who will listen; to be honest and candid about the good, bad and ugly of my past. Through God and the Savior's grace, the support of a wife who has taught me what it means to be truly Christlike, and a lot of hard work, I am healing. Amid all the pain, sorrow, anguish and hurt, I've found a silver lining. I have many callings in life, but helping others find healing for themselves, their families and their marriages is among the most significant to me. By initially seeking recovery in all the wrong ways, I've learned through personal experience, education and professional training how to help others heal.

There is Hope for You

I hope that my experience, both personally in my recovery journey as well as professionally in helping clients to find healing, can also help you find hope and the courage to confront your addiction. Change and recovery are possible; life becomes worth living.

I hope this book helps you see that "the sun will come up." Don't give up. There is still hope. There always will be. You are not too far gone. You are not beyond the reach of Christ's atoning sacrifice. People can change. Relationships can be healed. Wounds can be treated and hearts can be mended. We, and those we humbly reference in the following pages, are testaments of this. Please know that if we can do it, anyone can. Read on to learn how recovery has worked for us, how it is working in the lives of our clients, and how it can work for you.

MY STORY BY MARK KASTLEMAN

Exhausted and utterly spent from hours of quietly sobbing in my dimly lit garage, I stood staring indifferently at the .45 caliber pistol resting silently on the middle shelf of my gun safe. It would be a simple thing to press the cold barrel against my temple, pull the hair trigger and finally put an end to the interminable decades of ceaselessly trying and always failing. A thousand times I had vowed to stop using pornography, and a thousand times I betrayed everyone and everything I cared about. Surely my family, friends and the world would be far better off without a weak, pathetic loser like me. I reached out to grasp hold of the smooth, black grip and then, I hesitated. Something or someone gently held me back. A glimmer of hope sparked in my empty, broken heart and reason surfaced in a terribly troubled mind as I backed away and quietly closed and locked the heavy door.

It was 1995 and I was living with my wife and six children in a rented home in a quaint little town near the southern California coast. I was broke and unemployed with no viable prospects or visible paths forward. For more than twenty years I had been secretly and hopelessly shackled by sexual addiction, all the while remaining active and dedicated to my LDS faith. Finally on that fateful night,

I was unwilling to live any longer with the endless secrecy, duplicity and hypocrisy. Worn and spent from the perpetual roller coaster of fighting and giving in, overcoming and falling back, I came within a whisper of implementing a desperate and irreversible solution. Yet, through what I would come to recognize as God's loving intervention and grace, my life was not done.

Today I'm sober and happily married to the love of my life, my sweetheart of 37 years; passionate in the privilege of being a father and grandfather; active in my high priest's quorum and serving in church callings. I regularly attend the temple and humbly and gratefully look for opportunities to lift, love and serve as a disciple of Jesus Christ. From moment to moment, I rely wholly upon the Savior's love, power and grace to stay sober and keep moving forward.

So how exactly did I get to that dark and hopeless place in 1995? It began a couple of decades earlier as a shy, terribly insecure, deeply troubled teen living in the San Fernando Valley—the pornography production capital of the world.

Pornography—Hooked in an Instant

On a hot summer afternoon, standing in a sweltering attic, I huddled in a tight circle with the guys from my teachers quorum. We were engaged in a service project helping our bishop repair and clean one of his rental properties. In the process, an abandoned Playboy magazine was discovered. The word passed quickly and everyone slipped into the attic to grab a peek. We all gawked and giggled until finally the magazine was discarded and everyone stealthily slipped back to their respective tasks. Everyone that is, except me.

Earlier, while standing in that circle, I was completely mesmerized by the airbrushed images, which had a singularly powerful, deeply intoxicating effect on me. I pretended to leave with the rest of the group, but then secretly returned to retrieve the glossy publication. As I crouched down to take hold of it, my hands trembled. I quickly ripped out and folded the most provocative pages and nervously concealed them in my back pocket. This simple act would start a cascade of events that would impact the remainder of my life in ways I could not possibly imagine.

I had already become dependent on masturbation as my escape for self-soothing whenever life became unmanageable or unbearable. But pornography added an intensity and magnification of feeling for which I was entirely unprepared. The pure pleasure rush was immense, but it was much more than that. In a strange and powerful way the images made the ugly, awkward, unworthy "me" feel accepted and desired. For three weeks I held onto those images and used them for continual self-medication. From that time forward, I was hopelessly hooked.

Living in the San Fernando Valley, pornographic magazines were readily accessible in neighborhood bookstores, gas stations, corner drugstores and even the local grocery store. Yes, there were laws against minors viewing these materials, but managers often looked the other way or I would simply sneak them to a restroom or other secluded part of the store. This constant influence led to a cycle of obsessive/compulsive sexual thoughts and behaviors that dominated my teenage years.

My Shackles of Shame

While I constantly struggled with sexual addiction, I also continued to be active in my LDS faith. I attended all of my Sunday meetings, participated in Young Men's activities, was active in church sports and Scouting, readily volunteered for service projects, fulfilled callings and leadership positions, and by all outward signs, appeared to be the "model Mormon." But in reality, I was living two very distinct lives. I was the epitome of the proverbial *Dr. Jekyll and Mr. Hyde*—teen version.

There was one thing I feared more than dying—the discovery and sure-to-follow broadcasting of my secret sexual behaviors. On the outside I appeared to have it all together. But on the inside I was choked by a flood of self-doubt, fear, unworthiness, insecurity, self-loathing and a host of related emotions, all swarming together in that toxic hive known as *shame*. I didn't simply make mistakes; I was a mistake. I didn't just do bad things; I was bad, hopelessly flawed and broken. The only thing that offered any sense of worth or value in my fragile soul was my outward appearance and reputation. If I could gain the affections and affirmations of others by putting on a facade, at least that was something to hold on to. To lose that was to lose everything!

I went to great lengths to hide my addiction. I lied to my parents and my bishop. I engaged in secretive, stealthy and even elaborate practices and rituals to keep my sexual acting out hidden from family, friends, ward members and my peers. I had a firm belief in God and the restored gospel. My heart was filled with sincere desires to do good and be worthy, but no matter how much I resisted sexual urges, I always ended up giving in. And with every failure my sense of hypocrisy, duplicity and worthlessness deepened. Shame was my near-constant companion, and that pain was often the catalyst that drove me to escape and self-soothe through my addiction; each fueled the other. I was trapped in a downward spiral!

The Miracle of a Mission

The summer following high school graduation was a dark and depressing time. I was floundering deep in addiction with no direction or hope for the future. Then, through what I would later recognize as a series of tender mercies and divine intervention, I found myself at BYU as a freshman rooming with five returned missionaries. Their examples and mentoring had a profound effect on me. About that same time, I met and began dating an extraordinary young woman, also a freshman, whose eternal optimism, unconditional love and kindness changed my life.

I sought out my bishop and stake president and began the frightening and amazing process of full disclosure and the path of repentance and forgiveness. The following year I was called on a full-time mission to Sydney Australia, Spanish speaking. It was the most grueling, rewarding and remarkable experience of my life to that point. Through tremendous mental exertion, powered and sustained by the grace of Christ and the Holy Spirit, I was able to remain almost entirely free of unwanted sexual behaviors. There were occasional struggles with masturbation, and some second glances at the publicly displayed pornography in Sydney, but for one with my sexual addiction history, it was nothing less than miraculous!

I worked hard, developed a deep love for the people and learned firsthand about the diverse gifts and workings of the spirit and the literal power of the holy priesthood. Through divine inspiration and revelation I received a sure witness, repeated many times, of the reality of my Heavenly Father and His beloved Son, the prophet Joseph Smith, the Book of Mormon and the restoration. It was an honor and privilege for which I will be forever grateful.

I returned home filled with hope and optimism, taking for granted that all my addiction tendencies and struggles were a thing of the past and I could move forward with peace and confidence.

The Roller Coaster Ride from Hell

Not long after arriving home, my BYU sweetheart and I were sealed in the Los Angeles Temple. I was on cloud nine; life was very near perfect! Six months later we were living in Salt Lake City. I was attending college full time, holding down a job, serving in an elders quorum presidency and we were expecting our first child. Finances were extremely tight and the stress and pressure were enormous. Without warning, I was blindsided by the last thing I expected. After more than three years of freedom from addiction, it reared its ugly head with a vengeance!

As my stress increased, so did the old sexual urges and cravings. I was shocked by their extreme intensity and how it all began to consume my thoughts and interfere with every aspect of my life. It felt like I was back in high school; like it never left me. I was scared, frustrated and angry, and I was ashamed. No returned missionary newly married in the temple and soon to be a father should be having these thoughts and struggles! What was wrong with me? Why was I so weak and perverted?

I went to war with my sexual thoughts and urges; I fought them until finally, battle-worn and exhausted, I gave in and viewed pornography. That fateful choice unleashed a cascade of sexual addiction, secrecy, duplicity, depression and deep pain that would endure for more than 20 years. Endlessly fighting and giving in, overcoming and falling, hundreds of times, until completely exhausted, hopeless and broken, I stood in a dimly lit garage in southern California reaching for the pistol that would end my misery; that would finally get me off the roller coaster ride from Hell. Thankfully, miraculously, God had a different idea about how I was to eventually regain my freedom.

God Sends an Angel

On a beautiful Sabbath morning in the River Bottoms community of Provo, Utah, I sat comfortably with an intimate group of friends and colleagues. From the front of the room a kind, confident, powerful voice seemed to resonate with every cell in my body. It was as if the windows of heaven had opened and pure light, knowledge and understanding were flowing into my mind and heart. I excitedly scanned the room and wanted to shout, "Are you hearing this?! Do you understand the magnitude of what this man is sharing?!"

It was about a year after my near-suicide when I received a special invitation to attend a scripture-study gathering led by Dr. Page Bailey, a world-renowned neuropsychologist and passionate Baptist who was on a lecture tour in Utah. As I sat enraptured, hanging on his every word, I heard for the first time in my life a logical, beautiful, scientific and spiritual explanation for "why" I was hopelessly, shamefully trapped in sexual addiction! Decades of darkness and confusion began to disperse, replaced by the beginnings of light and clarity. For the first time, I felt real hope and the possibility of a path forward.

Over the next few years, Dr. Bailey became my teacher, mentor and like a second father. Under his wise and loving tutelage, I plunged into the fascinating and often overwhelming world of the science and psychology of the brain, human behavior and addiction. After three years of intensive study and research, I authored my first book, *The Drug of the New Millennium: The Brain Science Behind Internet Pornography Use.* Dr. Bailey and I were pioneers, among the first to claim that pornography radically alters the brain and literally creates a *chemical dependency* in many ways identical to the effects of street drugs. From that time forward I knew I had found my true calling. I left my career in the financial world to focus my time, energy and resources on my own recovery and helping others shackled in the chains of the insidious tyrant known as *pornography and sexual addiction.*

Recovery is a Journey, not a Destination

It would be natural to assume that the guidance of a world-renowned neuropsychologist, and volumes of newly acquired knowledge and understanding would be enough to free me from the bonds of addiction. There was a steady and remarkable change in me. I enjoyed longer periods of sobriety than I had since my mission. I felt the enormous weight of shame and unworthiness beginning to lift.

For the first time in 20 years I was not consumed 24/7 by a constant battle with sexual thoughts and urges. I actually began to have days and even weeks living like a "normal" man. I could feel my agency returning. It was pure elation and I was hopeful that the worst was behind me, with clear sailing ahead.

It was with great disappointment, frustration and anger toward God that I found myself still shackled in the chains of sexual addiction. Was I enjoying longer periods of sobriety? Yes. Did I often feel free from sexual obsession and preoccupation? Yes. Did I have knowledge and tools that were helpful? Yes. Then why did I still have periods of relapse where I would fall back into old behaviors? I thought I was finally free of this hellish curse! What was I missing? Why did God refuse to take this from me?!

In those early days of recovery, I possessed a deep intellectual knowledge of the science and internal workings of my brain and behaviors. I believed that if I could gain sufficient knowledge and become proficient in the use of certain psychological tools, I would one day be "cured" of my addiction and then I could live a happy, normal life. I had yet to understand and internalize three all-important principles:

1. **Sexual addiction is only a symptom.** I must be willing to uncover, work through and heal the underlying core causes of my sexual addiction behaviors. For me, these have included:

religious shame, fears, anger, self-doubt, self-loathing, emotional immaturity, selfishness, childhood traumas, avoidance and escape, arrogance, a false image of God, isolation, difficulty with real intimacy, a surface and skewed understanding of grace and the Atonement, and many more. Once I began working on these core issues, as opposed to focusing all my attention and efforts on the symptoms, my progress was greatly accelerated.

2. **Recovery is a journey, not a destination.** My recovery is a beautiful life-long, upward-spiraling journey of learning, growing and healing. I can embrace and be grateful for every step along the way. Now, recovery is simply a natural part of my daily routine, and it is a treasured blessing in my life.

3. **Of myself, I am powerless over this addiction.** It is only yoked with Christ, enabled and empowered by His love and grace that I can daily do the things necessary to live in freedom, peace and joy. Through my religious culture and a lifetime of incorrect interpretation, I possessed a very surface and skewed concept of grace through the Atonement of Christ. Once I understood and embraced God's unconditional love and acceptance, and learned how to draw upon the enabling power of grace to work on my daily recovery, my progress surged forward!

If We Can, So Can You!

As Steve and I travel our own personal recovery paths and labor in love to help others hopelessly shackled in sexual addiction, we are often asked, "Is there any real hope for me?" "Can I truly be free from this hellish curse?" "I have done so many dark and shameful things. Can I ever be clean and accepted by God?"

Our resounding response without hesitation is, "YES!" We are completely confident that you can do it because you are NOT alone! We, and so many like us, know the deep, dark pit of sexual addiction. We know what it's like to hopelessly battle this relentless foe for decades. And we also know the precious peace and joy of real, lasting recovery and freedom! If we can do it, so can you!

If you decide to take the plunge and fully commit yourself to your recovery and healing journey, you will join a sacred brotherhood of striving LDS men who successfully walk the recovery path every day. It will be perhaps the most difficult, stretching and testing work you have ever done. But armed with the right knowledge, tools, practices and support, and sustained moment-to-moment by the love, grace and power of Christ, we truly can do all things!

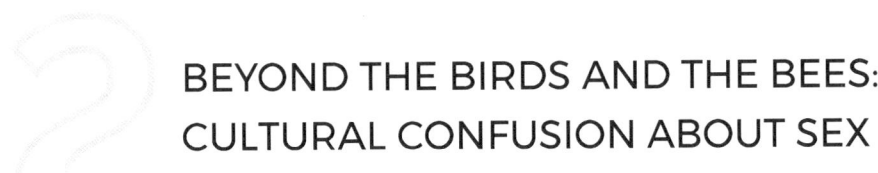

BEYOND THE BIRDS AND THE BEES: CULTURAL CONFUSION ABOUT SEX

Stephen Moore

To unravel the complexity of sex and pornography addiction (pornography addiction is really a subset of sexual addiction), we must first recognize the societal and cultural "causes and conditions" behind it, along with its power and impact. Several cultural components play a role in a person's vulnerability to sexual addiction.

A Critical Subject We Rarely Talk About

Sexuality is a core element of our internal identity, both as individuals and as members of the human race, and plays an integral role in a person's life. As a powerful means of both expressing and exploring connection in our most intimate relationships, it is the ultimate Godlike act that we experience in mortality. It allows us to partake in the purest form of creation, both of life as well as intimacy and love. For most Latter-day Saints, it's also a subject rarely discussed openly, even within marriage. If you are married, ask yourself: "When was the last time I really talked about sex with my partner? When was the last time I explored what sex means to us? For that matter, when was the last time I considered what sex means to me?"

This lack of communication is even more common in the

relationship between parents and children, as well as between teens and ecclesiastical leaders. In working with clients, several common themes regarding communication are nearly universal. One is the lack of real discussion about sex with their parents while growing up. While some men remember having "the talk" with their parents at some point, many are not able to recall a single instance where sex was openly discussed, other than being told "don't do it until you're married." Most of these men grew up in homes where sex was, at best, an awkward topic, and more commonly, not discussed at all. This is one of the cultural commonalities about sex that help "set the stage" for sexual confusion in general, and for some, an addiction they never anticipated.

Because It is Sacred, Must It also be Secret?

The "healthiest" discussions about sex I recall having prior to the early stages of my addiction both happened in rapid succession. The first occurred at the "maturation night" that was held at my local elementary school when I was 10- or 11-years-old. It was a blur of diagrams about anatomy, the importance of abstinence, and "saying no" to sex. After the presentation, each boy was given a small deodorant bar and the girls were given feminine hygiene products. I left more confused and with more questions than when I arrived.

The second discussion came a short time later, when my father sat me down to have "the talk" about sex. He was a business executive and a leader in the LDS Church. I had seen him comfortably give speeches to large crowds and confront subordinates at work. He was comfortable talking with friends or strangers about a wide variety of topics.

He took me to my parents' bedroom (which only occurred when I was in trouble), said all the right things and was as open as he could be. What I remember most is how uncomfortable he looked. I had never seen him so nervous about anything in my life. As the discussion ended, he said, "If you have any questions, you can always come and talk to me." While well-meaning, my father's demeanor taught me more about the subject of sex than anything he said. I walked away knowing I would never ask him anything about it. My young mind determined that sex was to be discussed only in the most solemn circumstances, and wasn't something people should open up about. Such experiences can create the underpinnings of secrecy early on for those who find themselves caught in the addiction cycle. Yet this is precisely when early intervention might be the most effective. Instead, sexual compulsion becomes a secret that must be protected at all costs. As actions grow into addiction, the secrecy grows too.

Is Sex the Enemy?

"Tim" (not his real name) and his wife had made significant progress in healing from addiction, both individually and as a couple. But as time passed, a problem they were not expecting arose: they were trying to bring sexual activity back into their marriage, but had difficulty doing so. Up to that point Tim believed his past "overindulgence" in sex was part of what had contributed to his addiction. As we explored his feelings of hesitation, however, it became apparent that Tim carried a lot of shame. During years of battle, he had come to view not just the addiction, but his sexuality as the enemy.

We spent significant time exploring these feelings, trying to separate his addiction from his sexuality. This entailed helping Tim understand that his sexuality wasn't "good or bad," but that using it to numb difficult emotions, avoid facing challenges, and emotionally regulate himself was toxic and destructive. His sexuality might best be viewed as a tool: a means to connect. The tool itself was not broken, but the way he had been using it for most of his life was.

Tim's story is not uncommon. Often, those struggling with sexual addiction are not aware that the addictive component is only the tip of the metaphorical iceberg. While a man may be aware of some problems surrounding his sexuality, it's not until he begins to address these problems that the deeper issues contributing to his addiction are exposed. Tim's struggles are an example of the complexity and deep inner workings of sexual addiction, including its culturally distorted origins.

My friends, *sex isn't the enemy.* Long-term recovery does not mean long-term abstinence. Quite the contrary! Sexuality is a beautiful gift from God; an amazing means of connection that can uniquely connect hearts and minds in the most intimate relationships. Used improperly, it will have the opposite effect: instead of a stronger connection with our spouse and our Creator, we experience self-loathing and shame, both of which result in a disconnection from others and God.

Clients often tell me, "I wish I didn't even have a sex drive; at least then, I would stop ruining my life and hurting the people around me!" I used to struggle with the same feelings and frustrations. In the depths of our addiction, it is difficult to not see sex as our enemy. Often, clients initially feel that sex is their problem. They plead, "Just help me stop acting out!" One client in particular comes to mind. We were discussing the emotional and spiritual process that is part of recovery from sexual addiction. Somewhat confused, he said to me, "Look, I don't really want to work on that emotional stuff! I didn't come here to talk about my feelings; I came to figure out how to quit hurting my wife!" He had the feeling many do when they first begin their recovery journey—that sex is the problem.

Believe me when I say, *Sex is not your problem; the way you're using it is.* The addiction itself is only a symptom. Just as with any disease, treating the symptoms is helpful, but without addressing the core issues themselves, long-term recovery is impossible. In future chapters we will help you address not just your addiction, but also its underlying causes.

OUR SEX-SATURATED SOCIETY IS A SET-UP!

Mark Kastleman

To really examine the *pornography paradox*—how and why LDS men can become trapped in pornography and sexual addiction—we must acknowledge that part of the explanation involves what we call the *grand setup*.

The magnificent human brain is divinely designed to be extremely efficient. And one of its most effective tools for efficiency is the use of simple repetition to create habits. Repeat a thought, a phrase or an action long enough and eventually it becomes automatic. It's through this application of consistent practice that we learn, grow and progress.

Imagine what would happen if each time we tried to walk, speak, tie our shoes or engage in any other common habit, we had to master it all over again? Without the power of habits, we wouldn't get very far in life. And once a habit is in place, the brain stamps it with "mission accomplished" and vigilantly guards what it has worked so hard to learn and to earn. No wonder it's so tough to lose weight, eat healthy, control anger or break out of any long-standing negative habits!

While some habits are created through conscious effort, others are formed in the semi-conscious or unconscious repetitions of our daily lives. Whether we realize it or not, a significant number of our sexual attitudes, feelings and understandings have been learned in the daily *sex education class* of the school we call popular culture.

A Constant Bombardment

Every man I've helped on the path to overcoming sexual addiction can trace the origins of his struggle back to powerful sexual influences, which nearly always began at a young age. One client I'll call "Sam," expressed it this way:

> As far back as I can remember I've lived in a culture filled with sexualized images and messages. As a kid growing up in the '80s and '90s, it was a rare day when my eyes or ears didn't take in some kind of sexual content from stuff that was pretty subtle and a lot that was just plain graphic. It came from TV sitcoms and other popular programs, and even commercials. I heard it in music lyrics and saw it in music videos. It was in Hollywood movies, advertising and on billboards. Sex was a big part of popular jokes and comedy routines. I even saw sexual images on magazine covers at the grocery store checkout. And of course, being a really observant kid, I picked up a lot on the sexual attitudes, conversations, behaviors and clothing styles of the people around me.
>
> But as bad as the '80s and '90s were, they don't hold a candle to where we are today. All the stuff I grew up with is still there, but now there's a whole lot more! With the Internet, video games, social media, online dating and hookup sites, and now virtual reality, anything and everything imaginable and unimaginable is instantly available in the palm of your hand at the push of a button. It's simply in your face all the time. For those of us who struggle with addiction, it all just gets to the point of being completely overwhelming.

The Rewired Brain

If the brain learns through repetition, and repetition builds habits, imagine the impact of being immersed daily in a sexualized society! I often ask clients in my group recovery programs to, "Think back on your life and try to estimate how many sexual images, ideas and messages have assaulted your eyes and ears, and in turn, have been stored in your brain's memory banks." Beginning at the age of 10 for a man now age 40, assume just two exposures to some type of sexual messaging per day. The total number of messages exceeds 20,000! Based on the realities of the society we live in, I invite you to calculate the actual number throughout your life experience.

I believe that human sexuality is of divine design, a beautiful and precious gift from our Heavenly Father. I believe He purposefully wired the human brain and body to experience sexuality in a healthy, passionate and powerful way. Expressed and enjoyed within the safety of His all-loving, all-wise ways, this wondrous power brings myriad blessings to the marriage relationship. Yet, in too many cases, years of constant bombardment and repetition can rewire the brain and set us up for sexual obsession, compulsion and addiction.

The Grand Setup

A logical observation at this juncture might be: "Mark, we've all grown up in this sexualized society, but we're not all suffering with sexual addiction."

We may be tempted to explain sexual addiction as a simple moral failing, lack of willpower, defect of character, act of rebellion or a conscious decision to abandon one's faith, family and covenants. In my experience, it's never that simple.

When a brain has been rewired through exposure to tens of thousands of sexual messages and images over years or decades (the grand setup), that brain is often a fertile seedbed just waiting for the right set of conditions for sexual obsession, compulsion and addiction to sprout. Addiction can be triggered in early childhood, the teen years, young adulthood, or can lay dormant and spring up in later adult years.

The contributing and triggering conditions are as varied as the men who find themselves trapped. How and why certain conditions can lead to addiction will be examined in great detail later in this book. For now, think of the brain as a vigilant scanning system searching for any signs of discomfort or potential danger; seeking instant, effective solutions for escape and self-soothing. The greater the discomfort or perceived threat, the more immediate and potent the solution sought by the brain. From a neurochemical standpoint, pornography and other sexual addiction outlets are among the most powerful means for self-medication on the planet!

For me, and my many clients over the years, triggers for self-medication, self-soothing and escape have included things like: childhood trauma and abuse; feelings of shame and unworthiness; depression and anxiety; some aspects of religious culture and doctrinal distortions; work or family stress; mental illness; health challenges; social phobia; exposure to pornography; a subtle cascade of poor choices; and a host of others. The point is, given the right conditions and a few poor choices, there's no telling who might be vulnerable and could fall into the trap.

The Great Miracle

It is no accident that you and I live in a fallen world at this particularly challenging time in history. Our Heavenly Father knew He was sending us to a time and place where we would be constantly bombarded by sexual messages, images and temptations. He knew this would have a detrimental impact, even a rewiring effect on the fallen human brain. And in His foreknowledge, He prepared a way for us to be rescued and fully healed. In fact, He placed part of His loving solution right into the very structure of the human brain itself.

In Romans 12:2 we read, *"And be not conformed to this world: but be ye transformed by the renewing of your mind, that ye may prove what is that good, and acceptable, and perfect, will of God."*

In our day, we call this divinely-designed, built-in ability of the brain to be transformed and renewed: *neuroplasticity*. God made the magnificent human brain moldable, shapeable and changeable—*plastic*. While this sexualized world can rewire the brain, it can also be transformed, renewed and restored to healthy wiring, healthy sexuality, healthy relationships and a joyful life. And where do the men trapped in addiction find the enabling power that makes this all possible? It is in and through the love, grace and Atonement of the Lord Jesus Christ; but more on that later.

SEXUAL SHAME IN A RELIGIOUS CULTURE

Stephen Moore

As we discussed in chapter 3, it's an understatement to say that our views on sexuality have been significantly influenced by popular culture. Media of all varieties has done much to diminish the sacredness and significance of human sexuality. Yet, there is another less-recognized influence that can play a significant part in distorting gospel principles and fundamental truths about the sacred role and nature of sexuality. It comes from a source that has a heavy influence on how we view the physical, emotional and spiritual ramifications regarding sex: our religious culture itself.

Contaminated Candy

Over the years, many of my clients have shared some of the influences of *religious culture* that have significantly impacted how they view themselves and their sexuality. One client shared the following account:

> I was a teenager sitting in a combined Young Men's and Young Women's lesson on the law of chastity. The teacher had a big bag of hard candy in individual wrappers. He passed one piece to each class member. He whispered something to one of the young men

and then invited all of us to unwrap and eat the candy. We all did except the one young man.

The teacher then proceeded to compare those of us eating the candy to people who participate in premarital sex, and the one boy whose candy was still in its wrapper was likened to those who save themselves sexually for marriage. Then we were instructed to remove the candy from our mouths and put it back into the wrapper. The teacher then asked whether a future spouse would choose the contaminated candy, or candy that had not been licked or chewed.

From that time on I believed that if I ever had any kind of improper sexual behavior it would permanently damage my virtue, value and worth. This was a seed planted early in my impressionable young mind that contributed to my later struggles with shame and sexual addiction.

Shame: A Principle as Old as Sin

Shame, particularly sexual shame, began with Adam and Eve, whom God created and placed in the Garden of Eden where sin did not exist. Genesis 2:25 records that *"... they were both naked, the man and his wife, and were not ashamed."* As the story progresses in scripture, Satan plays a role in removing Adam and Eve's innocence around many things, including their sexuality. After the two partake of the forbidden fruit, Satan turns the tables on them. Genesis 3:7-10 records that *"... the eyes of them both were opened, and they knew that they were naked... And the Lord God called unto Adam, and said unto him, where art thou? And he said, I heard thy voice in the garden, and I was afraid, because I was naked, and hid myself."* Thus shame—both as a core concept, and specifically related to sexuality itself—was first introduced by the adversary among God's children.

Terminal Uniqueness: Am I Beyond Saving?

Much research and writing has been done about the general concept of shame, but for our purposes, it's important to differentiate a few key components of *shame*, specifically with regard to its emotional cousin, *guilt*. We feel guilt when we do something contrary to what we believe is right. Guilt can be viewed as our conscience, the Light of Christ, the Holy Ghost, etc. Guilt is a healthy, God-given blessing, in that it inspires and drives us to make change. Guilt is a negative feeling, but necessary as a primary means of personal growth. Guilt (understood in our context to be "healthy" guilt) helps a person recognize that mistakes and sins are part of his life, but they don't define him.

Shame, on the other hand, twists guilt in such a way that mistakes and sins are viewed as one's *identity*, rather than as choices that can be changed and repented of. In other words, shame about being a sex addict often tells that person he is broken, defective and weak. He believes his addiction is not simply a weakness to be conquered; rather, *it is an identity he must conceal.*

As I mentioned previously, in the course of my addiction history, I eventually began preparing to serve an LDS mission. I was able to gain a sufficient length of "sobriety" from acting out in my addiction that I was deemed ready to serve. While on my mission, I experienced a significant reduction in my sexual acting out for many reasons, though I continued to occasionally struggle with it, and worked with priesthood leaders in combating it as best I could. But the shame-based identity that I carried as an individual, in part defined by my sexual deviancy and history, continued to play a dominant role in the way I viewed myself.

During my missionary service, one person I taught who was interested in joining the church shared a large list of mistakes that most members would consider to be extremely serious, including a long history of sexual indiscretion. During one discussion, she proceeded to lay out her "sinful past" to us, describing how she would never be worthy to join the church because of her past actions. I remember teaching with spiritual power, testifying that she could, in fact, be forgiven. I absolutely believed this and felt a spiritual confirmation of what was being taught, yet I remember thinking, "But this doesn't apply to me; I should know better. I have the truth, but I keep doing these things. I am beyond the power of the Atonement."

For those unacquainted with the mindset of someone overcome

with shame, this thought process may sound foreign. To someone who struggles with such feelings, however, this reasoning is unsettlingly familiar. A belief in "terminal uniqueness"—the idea that one's own actions are so extreme that they fall outside the bounds of "normal" rules like the Atonement—is crippling to an addict. *His shame tells him he cannot change, that he is beyond saving* and that somewhere along the trail of addiction, he crossed a point of no return and is now fundamentally broken. His shame, and its consequent sense of hopelessness, increases as he continues to make valiant attempts to stop his sexual acting out, only to fail again. Addicts who fall into this trap begin to believe, with each new failure, that they really cannot change; thus, the shame they feel around their sexuality begins to deepen, and their hope and desire to change diminishes.

In my experience, this shame-based perspective forms the bedrock of hopelessness for nearly every addict. It is also one of the most frustrating and nebulous concepts for their loved ones. For those not mired in such distorted thinking, it can be nearly impossible to understand this mindset. Even worse, those who try to support the addict most are at risk of perpetuating and deepening their loved one's shame as they ask—either verbally or mentally—"Why won't you just stop?" They perceive the addict's behavior as incredibly selfish. Consequently, addicts often end up distancing themselves from the very support system they desperately need to find hope and healing.

Addicts live in a complex emotional space, mired with feelings of hopelessness, shame, regret and self-loathing. They have occasional moments of euphoria as they attempt to cope with it all through acting out in their addiction. These "highs," however potent for the addict, are never long-lasting. They don't alleviate the symptoms. Instead, they mask the symptoms of dysfunction by acting as a numbing agent upon which the addict becomes increasingly dependent. He is caught in the endless cycle of *using his problem as a temporary solution.* He becomes more desperate each time he experiences relief followed by the inevitable crash.

WE'RE OUTSIDE CHRIST'S CIRCLE, TRYING TO EARN OUR WAY BACK IN

Mark Kastleman

"Mark, I despise myself for looking at porn and masturbating. It goes against everything I hold dear, everyone that matters to me, but I just keep doing it! I get so frustrated and confused by my choices that I want to scream until my lungs explode! I hate myself so deeply there are times when I just want to end it all. God must be so fed up and disgusted with me. It's amazing He hasn't taken me out by now."

MINGLED WITH SOBS, these heart-rending words came gushing forth from the tear-stained face of a big, strong LDS man as he slumped down broken and hopeless in my counseling office. Those who knew him—his family, work colleagues and ward members—would not have recognized him. From his everyday outside appearance, he seemed to have it all together—successful businessman, "ideal" marriage and family, trim and fit, active in ward callings, popular and well-liked. But in the hidden chambers of his mind and heart, in the stealthy behaviors of his secret addiction, lived an entirely different man. The constant Jekyll and Hyde-like battle, the ever-present contrast, conflict and duplicity, left him worn and battle-weary.

All of us who have struggled with unwanted sexual behaviors and addiction know this man's story all-too-well. Some of us continue living our double lives, going to every length to maintain our masks, facades and secrecy. Others have been discovered or have come forward voluntarily, often making some progress, only to relapse or remain trapped in addiction. All the while, we are *living contradictions*—feeling intensely attracted and allured by that which also brings overwhelming feelings of deep regret, self-loathing, disgust and self-hatred.

The Shame that Binds Us

Living a double life brings us to the place where we suffer from what is perhaps the most toxic emotion on earth—*shame*. When an emotionally and spiritually healthy individual makes a poor choice, they feel a sense of *guilt*, which creates discomfort and sends the clear message, "I made a mistake; I recognize it, admit it, make amends if needed, learn from it, make some adjustments and move forward." This is God's loving gift of a *conscience*, the *light of Christ* within each of us, designed to help us recognize when we're off the path of love, peace and happiness. It prompts and motivates us to learn from our mistakes and use them as stepping-stones to move forward.

Shame is an entirely different beast. While healthy guilt gently and firmly reveals, "I made a mistake," shame emphatically shouts, "I am a mistake! I am inherently bad, flawed and broken. I am unworthy of love, acceptance or belonging." Feelings of guilt through Christ's light illuminate our experiences and help us see more clearly the lessons to be learned and the path forward. Shame, at the opposite extreme, is an emotion first introduced by Satan himself and easily conjured up by the fallen brain. It is a darkness that obscures the truth and blocks the way ahead.

Unfortunately, there are certain aspects of our religious *culture* that tend to cultivate and amplify shame. When LDS men fall prey to the insidious trap of pornography, masturbation and other unwanted sexual behaviors, this creates within us a deep sense of shame, unworthiness and self-loathing. Many of us were raised in a family/religious culture where, for a host of different reasons and influences, we developed the perception of a stern, rigid, unforgiving and even vengeful *Old Testament God* anxious to punish us for our disobedience and shameful acts. Some of us felt this harsh attitude from our own fathers, mothers or other authority figures in our lives. One of my clients voiced it this way:

> *I always knew that God was up there just waiting for me to mess up one-too-many-times and then Whamo! Here comes fire from heaven to turn me into a pile of ash!*

Outside Christ's Circle

Over the decades of my own struggles with sexual addiction, I remember desperately trying to implement the solutions I believed I was hearing from my church leaders: pray, read your scriptures, be active, give service, etc. I interpreted these messages to mean that if I did these things consistently, God would deliver me from my addiction. I tried to comply with the counsel as best I could, and while I did make some temporary improvements, I always ended up slipping back into old, stubborn behaviors. At times, it seemed the harder I tried, the deeper I sank into my addiction. This caused me to seriously doubt my standing before God: to question His love, whether I had any real worth, and any hope of ever living free, let alone eventually making it to that highest degree of glory reserved for men far better than me. A close LDS friend described his similar journey this way:

> *During my decades of addiction I was told that all I had to do was sincerely turn to Christ and through His Atonement I would be able to break free. For endless years I tried to turn to Him the best I knew how—prayer, scripture reading, attending all my meetings and activities, serving others, attending the temple—but nothing gave me lasting freedom. I always slipped back into porn, masturbation and other sexual outlets. What church leaders were telling me to do didn't work for me!*
>
> *After what must have been a thousand failed attempts to break free, I finally came to the conclusion that I must somehow be outside Christ's circle of grace and help. The formula my church leaders were*

preaching must work for other addicts or why would they keep giving the same advice? If Jesus had the power to rescue me, why didn't He? I was obviously so far gone and perverted in my addiction, and Jesus so disappointed in me, that He was leaving me to be punished through endless struggle and failure. I realized that I was truly alone and on my own. I was permanently outside that blessed circle where Christ helped all the other addicts. Every relapse I had proved this to be true. I knew I would never be free.

A Real and Tangible Hope in Christ

If you can relate to the feeling of being "outside Christ's circle," don't despair. All of us in long-term, successful recovery were once where you are now. We didn't understand the all-important differences between *religious culture* and true *eternal doctrines*.

We believed that if we could muster sufficient willpower and sheer grit to remain free from sexually acting out long enough, we could then "earn" our way back into Christ's circle, His love and above all, His acceptance. We had committed to memory the often cited and well-worn scripture passage: *"for we know that it is by grace that we are saved after __all__ that we can do."*

While we could give impressive lessons and sacrament meeting talks about the Atonement, we had almost no understanding of the true enabling power and infinite reach of *grace*. We couldn't see that our real addiction was not to pornography and sex, but at the deepest level it was an addiction to our shame. We had isolated ourselves from others, from God and from our true, magnificent, *Eternal Selves*. In our recovery, we learned that the opposite of addiction is not sobriety, but rather "connection" and "oneness" with our true selves, others and God. We came to understand and know of a surety that we could never "earn" our way back into Christ's circle, for we were never outside it in the first place. He was always there, reaching out, loving and accepting us without condition, no matter what!

SEXUALLY OBSESSED: SEX AS A SUBSTITUTE FOR CONNECTION WITH OTHERS

Stephen Moore

I WAS RECENTLY TOLD about an advertisement depicting a scantily clad woman "washing a car" while holding a popular hamburger from a nationwide food chain. I didn't need to watch this particular commercial to understand the feel and tone. This company has been making such commercials for years, and their ads were one of many sources that fed my sexually addicted brain and behavior in the past. Suffice it to say that the commercial's emphasis has very little, if anything, to do with the food being advertised. In fact, the food itself is heavily sexualized. This ad and others like it reflect our increasingly sexualized culture. This cultural lens sets us up for sexually obsessive, and in many cases, sexually addictive behavior and thinking.

Sexuality is becoming a larger part of who is admired, respected, rewarded or accepted in our society. TV, movies and other media increasingly depict what they have determined is "normal" with regard to sex.

Sex as a Barometer of Worth and Connection

Sex is often depicted as the exclusive means of connecting with others. While sexuality is a potent and important means of connecting with our spouses and our spirituality, it is only one of many ways we can connect. It is increasingly commonplace for people to define the health of human relationships based on sexual activity and compatibility. "Sexual chemistry" is perceived to be more important than any other attributes; if the sex is good, then so must be the relationship. This cultural shift not only places more of a focus on a person's sexuality within a relationship, but does so at the expense of diminishing their personality and spiritual/emotional strengths. As the focus on the external increases, the importance of the internal evaporates. As sex increasingly becomes the premier barometer of one's value, it also becomes a measuring stick we hold our spouses to.

Sex is Connection, or is it?

Human beings are hard-wired to connect with others. We tend to thrive in connection and wither in isolation. The emphasis on sex as essential for good connection comes from a shift in sex as *a form of connection*, to sex as *a definition of the connection* in our most intimate relationships. This fallacy is perhaps best portrayed in pornography. The majority of pornography depicts people who find some sort of connection with each other, even if it is shallow. They then express that connection exclusively through sexual activity. This sets the stage for susceptibility to sexually addictive or compulsive behaviors, particularly for men who struggle with self-esteem. They find themselves lacking significant connection with other people. When the *myth*—"sex is the definition of connection," pairs with the *fact*—"we are hard-wired to connect with other people," it's clear why sexual addiction is an epidemic.

The cycle of sexual addiction begins with social and emotional isolation. A man who is emotionally compromised—without a support system to provide validation and acceptance—stumbles on sexual activity as a solution to his isolation and lack of self-acceptance. While engaging in sexual activity, he finds that many of these needs are (temporarily) met. As long as he is engaged sexually, he feels the connection he is so desperately seeking. His relief is temporary, and doesn't last much longer than the sexual activity itself. But in the moment, he feels elements of connection, including a sense of being desired, validated, respected and in control. Desperate for more, he is likely to act out in similar ways later on.

Dan's story represents this lack of connection:

> I remember being miserable as a child. My parents weren't close to us kids; looking back, I don't think I felt like I mattered much to them. I was shy as a kid; I didn't have many friends despite many efforts to make them. It was around that time that I had my first exposure to pornography. I will never forget the way I felt looking at those images. Here I was, a young man with no friends who felt like no one really cared about him, stumbling upon porn. Like most of us, I was sexually curious. I'm sure these images would have been tempting regardless of my own emotional headspace. I will never forget that first time: here were images of women—beautiful women—who were willing to be so open with themselves to me. Their willingness to be sexual with me, at least in my mind, caused me to feel loved and accepted in a way that I never had before. It was like a drug; I felt intoxicated. In that moment, I felt loved. Wanted. Desired.
>
> Looking back, I think I was hooked with that first exposure. I was desperate for love. I knew on some level that what I was doing was wrong, and I wanted to stop, but not really. I was desperate to be accepted and validated. And so I turned back to it again and again.

Is it Love or Lust?

Whole books could be written on the difference between "lust-based" sexual desire and what constitutes sexual desire based on genuine caring and connection. Every day I explore this concept with clients in my private practice. Lust and love are both nebulous, visceral feelings that are difficult to describe. For example, love is best identified not through description, but through experience. Love is so powerful it almost acts as a force of nature, yet it often defies description.

Discerning between lust and love is one of the most difficult concepts we must learn. Accurately distinguishing between the two often takes years. Here are a few rules I use in separating lust from love.

Lust:

- *Is primarily guided by our sexual drive.* Our biological and chemical makeup create within us a chemical and genetic drive to be sexual.
- *Is centered on self.* Lust is selfish by nature; it focuses on the needs of the self, even at the cost of the spouse's needs. How can I feel good? How can I use this situation to my own ends? How can this activity give me what I want? Other concerns are secondary to this. When we are caught in a lust-based mindset, we increasingly objectify those around us, including our spouses. People become little more than body parts, and their value is determined by how they can benefit us or not.
- *Is never satisfied.* When sex results from lust, one's connection with another is mimicked in many ways, but true connection is absent. Lust always needs increased novelty, newness and feelings of pleasure in order to be satisfied.

By contrast, *Love:*

- *Expresses an existing connection.* In healthy relationships, sex is the *unselfish* expression of connection, not an attempt to find connection exclusively through sex.
- *Is centered on the needs of the spouse.* The primary focus is not on form or types of pleasure, but on expressing love and desire for one's spouse and fulfilling their needs.
- *Is patient.* While lust often centers on the moment and struggles for instant gratification, love-based sexuality is focused on what is best for both partners. Because it is an expression of an existing emotional relationship, the immediate need and demand are not one's primary concern. In a loving partnership, sex is the natural progression of the developing relationship, rather than a simple mechanism for pleasure.

So long as sex continues to be lust-based, deep intimate connection with a spouse will be significantly hindered. Regardless of the quality of the sexual component, the relationship will feel hollow, unfulfilled and lacking. The more a man becomes attached to lust-based sex, the deeper his sexual compulsion runs, *impairing his ability to form healthy bonds.*

THE FUNNEL: THE SCIENCE BEHIND WHY WE ACT OUT SEXUALLY

Mark Kastleman

ANYONE WHO HAS battled sexual addiction knows the complete bewilderment and utter frustration with what I call *the great mystery*. Why do we repeatedly yield ourselves to the siren's call when it goes against everything we believe and hold dear? Why do we cast aside or ignore those we love most to narrowly and coldly pursue pleasure? Despite having endlessly vowed to never give in again, why do we continue making the same selfish, foolish, destructive choices? Here's how a close friend described his long experience with this baffling mystery:

> When my addiction urge would hit, it was like another totally separate person would take over. That guy didn't care about anyone or anything except his sexual goal. He was completely narrowed, calculating and unfeeling. When the acting out was done, it was like my real self would wake up and come back into focus. That's when the hell would always start. This condemning voice would shout in my head—"What have you done?" "What were you thinking?" "How could you have given in again?" "You're just a worthless pervert!" "You'll never be free of this!"
>
> No matter how much I analyzed it, pondered on it and broke it

down, I could never understand how I could become something so uncaring and cold. I would see it coming and try to resist and be strong, but it was relentless and ruthless and I usually ended up giving in to "that other guy." The confusion, frustration and self-hatred were overwhelming and brought me close to suicide several times.

I can so deeply relate to this good man's honest description! For decades, I too was buried in the frustrating confusion and utter mystery of my addiction. But through a series of miracles and divine interventions, God led to me to the man who would shine a guiding light in the darkness and help me solve *the great mystery*.

Dr. Page Bailey

It was fall, my favorite time of the year. I was on one of many calls with my teacher and mentor, neuropsychologist Dr. Page Bailey. With his home and headquarters in Portland, and my residence in Utah, we often had long conversations by phone.

The study topic that day was prompted by a simple query: "Page, why is it that so many good men can forget everyone and everything they care about under the influence of pornography and sexual temptation? Why is it so powerful?"

That was the day Dr. Bailey introduced me to the concept of *The Sexual Funnel*, which forever changed my understanding of my own addiction challenges, and in the years ahead, would become a foundational principle in all of my counseling, teaching and training work.

The Sexual Funnel

Imagine in your mind an hourglass, wide at the top and slowly narrowing down to a very small passageway in the center and then expanding to a wide opening at the bottom. This illustration can help you understand how the brain behaves during a sexual experience. As Dr. Bailey so often reminded me:

Mark, sexual climax is the most narrowly and powerfully focused biological event in which the brain can engage. This crescendo experience can only take place on a very narrow runway. In order to reach this place, the brain must narrowly focus its attention and block out all distractions. This is achieved in the Funnel.

When we feel sexually aroused and decide to pursue that urge, the brain immediately starts to narrow its focus as it releases a wave of internal chemicals, including: dopamine, testosterone, endorphins, norepinephrine, serotonin and oxytocin. These neurochemicals cause the brain to block out all distractions and focus full attention on the sexual process. They can also provide a host of positive benefits or extremely negative consequences, depending on how we choose to use the Funnel.

THE SEXUAL FUNNEL

Wide Perspective

Neurochemical Flood
&
Narrowing Focus

Tunnel Vision

Neurochemical Tidal Wave at Climax

Wide Perspective

The farther down the Sexual Funnel we travel, the more narrowly focused the brain becomes in its thinking and attention. The brain's primary goal is to eventually arrive at the very narrowest part of the

Funnel, sexual climax, where a final tidal wave of internal chemicals is released. After this crescendo experience, the neurochemicals dissipate and the brain returns to its wide perspective

One Funnel, Two Very Different Outcomes

God designed the Sexual Funnel experience to be highly intense and very powerful. Why? Because He needed his children to pro-create and form families. He also intended to give married couples a divine gift that would benefit and bless them in the myriad trials and opportunities of married life. To understand why the Funnel is so powerful, let's look at it from two very different perspectives—healthy marital intimacy and illicit sexual behaviors. While the same kinds of chemicals are released in both scenarios, the experience and especially the outcome are radically different. Viewing pornography will be used as just one example among a host of illicit sexual behaviors to which the Funnel principles can be applied.

Healthy Marital Intimacy: In a healthy marriage relationship, the Funnel experience causes husband and wife to focus narrowly on each other, block out the world and any negatives in the relationship. The Funnel creates a healthy dependency between husband and wife. Each spouse can remember the smallest details of their beloved's features, actions and cherished moments together. The special and sacred shared intimacy is locked in the memory and can be a strength and buoy during life's trials.

The Funnel experience forges a powerful bond between husband and wife, producing a feeling of oneness, closeness and attachment. This bond is as strong as the bond a mother and father have with their newborn child. The Funnel creates deep feelings of calmness, satisfaction and release from stress.

When husband and wife emerge from the narrow part of the Funnel, their wide perspective returns. The intimate experience leaves them feeling deeper love and appreciation, a stronger bonding and attachment, more fulfilled, energized, positive and better equipped to work individually and together to succeed in their overall lives and family responsibilities.

Pornography Viewing: With pornography use (and other illicit sexual behaviors) chemicals released during the Funnel experience cause the viewer to focus intensely and exclusively on the sexual images. His brain shuts out all other truth and reality, including thoughts of God, family, beliefs, consequences or future goals.

Because the Funnel creates temporary feelings of escape, self-soothing and release from the stress and pressures of life, it creates a powerful chemical dependency linked to the images.

The Funnel causes the brain to record and remember every sexual image with vivid clarity, years or even decades later, resulting in a constant, frustrating battle to eradicate them.

Many jump into the Funnel when they're feeling lonely, disconnected, emotionally needy and craving real human intimacy. Because the pornography experience is all fantasy, with no real human connection or sharing, the viewer is left feeling even more empty, lonely and wanting than before.

The Hopeless Dialogue

When the porn viewer emerges from the narrowest part of the funnel back to a wide perspective, his rational thinking returns and the *hopeless dialogue* begins: "What have I done? What was I thinking?"

The answer is, he wasn't—and in fact, couldn't—think. When he descends into the Funnel outside the safety of its divine purpose, he gives up his ability to "think." The overpowering flood of chemicals overrides his cognitive thought and reasoning abilities. "What about my wife, my children, my values, my covenants?" he pleads.

He can't believe how easily he has fallen yet again into the trap. He is hopeless in the face of his nemesis, his Goliath. How it all happened is a mystery to him. What he doesn't understand is that when he allows himself to enter the Funnel outside of marriage and pits his beliefs and commitments against one of the most powerfully focused and narrowed events the brain can experience—climax—his willpower fails every time!

PORNOGRAPHY USE IS SUBSTANCE ABUSE

Mark Kastleman

IN ADDITION to my work in the field of sexual addiction, it's been my privilege to counsel with courageous men and women who struggle desperately to overcome drug and alcohol abuse. Many have shared the fact that they also wrestle with some level of sexual obsession or addiction. What might surprise you is how many succeed in attaining sobriety from drug and alcohol use, but remain endlessly trapped in sexual addiction. Here's what one man in a substance abuse group openly shared:

> It was super tough to get clean from my heroin and alcohol use, but man I gotta say that the sexual stuff just won't let go. A lot of the situations and pressures where I used to go to drugs or drink to cope, I now find myself turning to porn and sex. And if I'm really honest about it, in some ways the rush or the high from the sexual acting out is more intense than the drugs. In fact I'd have to say from my experience that porn and sex are pretty much just like drugs, and for me actually harder to get over.

It might seem incredible that recovering addicts often describe struggles with unwanted sexual behaviors as more difficult to overcome than their drug use. Yet, now that you are familiar with the brain science behind the Sexual Funnel, it's not a difficult jump to make.

Yet, there are still some who cringe at labeling pornography and various other illicit sexual behaviors as "addictive" because they believe doing so affords an excuse: "I can't help myself, I'm addicted." Of course this is a preposterous position. When someone is addicted to alcohol, do we excuse his behavior because, "He can't help it?" Just because someone suffers with an addiction doesn't mean he doesn't have a choice. As you will discover in the second half of this book, there is <u>always</u> a choice when it comes to breaking free from addictive behaviors.

Can Sexual Behaviors Lead to a *Chemical Dependency?*

The more important question is not, "Are pornography and other sexual behaviors addictive?" but rather, "Can these behaviors lead to a *chemical dependency* commonly experienced with illicit street drugs, alcohol, tobacco, and prescription drugs?" Referring specifically to pornography, the question could be phrased, "Is pornography use substance abuse?"

Immediately, there are some scientific, medical and psychology experts who fire back, "How can you classify pornography as a drug or a substance? It doesn't come in a liquid, powder or pill form. You don't ingest it or inject it."

My response is two-fold:

1. When an individual ingests or injects a drug, that substance travels to the receptors in the brain and other parts of the body, seeking to mimic the body's own internal chemicals. In effect, the drug tries to "fake" the body into releasing its own natural or *endogenous* (meaning produced from within) chemicals. For example, Prozac triggers the body to release its own natural serotonin. Likewise, as you've seen from the Funnel illustration, pornography mimics sexual intimacy and fakes the body into releasing a tidal wave of endogenous chemicals, which is exactly what pharmaceutical and illicit street drugs do. Can pornography not then be referred to as a "drug?"

2. For those who insist on precision in the use of scientific terms such as "drug," allow me to put your minds at rest. Can we agree that pornography viewing and other illicit sexual behaviors trigger the release of the body's own endogenous chemicals? And that a person can become addicted to these internal chemicals just as he would if the release were triggered by a pharmaceutical drug? Is this not chemically-induced addiction?

Back in the late '90s I met a remarkable woman who would become a friend and mentor, Dr. Judith Reisman. I carefully studied Dr. Reisman's work as part of the research for my first book, *The Drug of the New Millennium: The Brain Science Behind Internet Pornography Use.* Judith was way ahead of her time; a watcher on the tower sounding the warning voice. For decades she worked closely with some of the best minds in neuroscience and neuropsychology to prove that pornography and other related sexual behaviors should, indeed, be considered a form of substance abuse and chemical dependency.

I remember a controversial (at the time) research paper she first produced in 2000 titled: *The Psychopharmacology of Pictorial Pornography, Restructuring Brain, Mind & Memory.* It was very technical, heavy reading, but once I grasped the reality of its message, the lights really came on. Here's an excerpt:

> A pornographic psychopharmacological flood yields epinephrine, testosterone, endorphins (endogenous morphine), oxytocin, dopamine, serotonin, phenylethylamine, and other pharmacological stimuli. In her book published by the Institute of Medicine, Sandra Ackerman notes that epinephrine alone gets the "vertebrate brain" "high" on its own self produced morphine or heroin. Pornography, designed to alert the procreation instinct to the need to immediately respond, would be especially likely to cause users to self-medicate, kick-starting these endogenous, adrenaline/norepinephrine, morphine-like neurochemicals for a hormonal flood, a "rush" allegedly analogous to the rush attained using various street drugs.

> *Arousal dependence [through pornography] may be compared to biochemical alterations related to excessive amphetamine use. Satiation effects [hours looking at Internet porn] may be compared to those related to opiate use. Fantasy behavior can be related to such neurotransmitters as dopamine, norepinephrine, or serotonin, all of which are chemically similar to the main psychedelic drugs such as LSD.*

A Public Health Crisis

It has been nearly two decades since Dr. Reisman and I, along with a few others, sounded the alarm regarding the immense power of pornography and related sexual outlets to create a literal chemical dependency/addiction in the brain akin to illicit street drugs. Many today still cling stubbornly to the antiquated claim that it's all just a "harmless pastime and recreational outlet." Yet, there's an increasing awareness and waking up to the truth.

In 2016, Utah legislators became the first elected officials to declare pornography usage a *public health crisis*. In fact, the state legislature unanimously passed a special resolution, which was signed by Governor Gary Herbert. The resolution detailed pornography's detrimental effects on brain function, its contribution to emotional and medical illnesses, and its role in deviant sexual arousal and behaviors. All of this brings great understanding and hope to those who struggle under the heavy burden of sexual addiction. I remember the early days of my work with Dr. Page Bailey and my first lessons about the Sexual Funnel, and the propensity of pornography to create a literal *chemical dependency* or *drug addiction* in the human brain and body. I cannot begin to express the hope I felt as the mists surrounding the *great mystery* began to clear. I was not hopelessly broken, flawed, weak and worthless. There was a logical, brain-science reason for my struggles! This knowledge was only the beginning of my journey to recovery.

AM I BEYOND SAVING?

Stephen Moore

BY NOW YOU ARE becoming familiar with some factors that are part of the addiction cycle, and how it perpetuates itself. This includes how the chemically and biologically-based sex drive can (to some degree) act as the never-ending "fuel" for addiction's "fire." On an emotional and spiritual level, sexual addiction is tied to a distorted belief that addicts begin to form early on: they are unable to change. Therefore:

Their sexual urges cannot be truly bridled in a healthy way.

Nothing can stop their addictive path.

They are beyond saving.

Such thoughts are self-perpetuating: the more they act out, the more their evidence-based brains begin to accept these distorted views and work against them. Each time an addict "gets up" to fight his addiction, only to be knocked down again, he begins to develop a habitual mentality. "I never change. No matter what I do, I always end up acting out again. It is not a question of *if* I will; it is only a question of *when* I will." Breaking this cycle of hopelessness is vital to recovery, and is a benefit of sobriety. Sobriety and small changes allow the addict to leave hopelessness behind and see that change may be possible.

Hungry for a Spiritual Connection

Earlier we explored how a lack of connection with others contributes to remaining stuck in addiction. Human wiring for connection extends far beyond simply connecting with others. We all have an inherent need to define ourselves; to discover the origins of our spiritual and eternal identity, and to know ourselves better through coming to know God. Life's universal questions—"Who am I?" "Where did I come from?" and "Where am I going?"—are answered in the relationship with God.

In sexual addiction, sex is often used to fill the gap that a man feels between God and himself. Using sexually compulsive behavior to fill this spiritual "God-hunger" is nearly universal among the men I work with. My own addiction fed off the perceived distance between God and me. At the time, I didn't feel wanted, accepted or loved by God. Though I was active in church—saying my prayers, reading scripture and religious study—I was becoming a whitewashed sepulcher on the outside while rotting spiritually within. I looked the part of a spiritually engaged man, but lacked a true connection with my Maker because of my own lack of self-worth, shame and guilt.

The pattern of using sex to fill the need for spiritual connection is a self-perpetuating problem that grows on its own. Addicts use sex to cope with their spiritual disconnection, and in turn feel shame and guilt. In order to escape these feelings, they fall back into destructive behaviors, which results in more of the negative feelings they were running from in the first place. This results in falling back into the same trap of acting out, and the addiction cycle is born: a never-ending loop of trying to escape from one's own feelings, shame and self-perceptions.

Sickness v. Defectiveness

I learned a phrase from a colleague that I often present to my clients: Are you a *sick man trying to become well*, or are you a *bad man trying to become good*? The question refers to two separate paradigms: the latter is based in one's own shame-driven identity, while the former hails from an accurate (although incomplete) view of one's spiritual self. "If

I am defective, how can there be help for me? I must be beyond even God's love and redemption."

As a therapist, I strongly feel that looking at one's self (or one's actions) as "good or bad" is a dangerous game for addicts who struggle with shame. That view can be distancing and destructive. Yet we use similar terminology in our church circles and congregations almost ubiquitously. While it's fair to say that one's actions might be "good" or "bad," addicts struggle to differentiate between *action and identity*. An addict not only sees his sexual acting out as "bad," but as proof that he is a bad person. Addicts believe to one degree or another that they are broken, flawed and defective.

"What is wrong with me?!" I have uttered this phrase myself countless times, often in a less-than-reverent demand for understanding, usually from God. I learned this phrase at an early age from a couple of very influential people in my life. While well-meaning, they were actually saying something incredibly destructive. This question implies that there is something about me that is fundamentally flawed. I have had client after client say this same phrase, or something like it, in my office countless times.

So long as an addict is caught in a cycle of believing that he is broken as a person, his addiction will continue to grow. After all, if the belief is true, what's the point of trying to change? I distinctly remember thinking this myself on several occasions in the past. *"What's the point?! If I am going to act out again eventually any way, I may as well give in to it! At least then I get some sort of enjoyment out of life! I may not like who I am, and the roller coaster to Hell is taking me further down no matter what I do, so I may as well enjoy the ride!"* Here again, it's difficult for someone outside of the addiction mindset to understand this logic, but in the shame-based world where addicts live, this is too often reality.

With each repeated attempt to control their addiction ending in failure, they increasingly come to view themselves through a hopeless lens. Any other viewpoint becomes a fantasy; something they have broken faith with too many times in the past to believe any longer. Hope begins to die.

SEXUAL ADDICTION IS NOT ABOUT SEX!

Mark Kastleman

"Mark, sexual addiction is not about sex," Dr. Page Bailey boldly declared during one of our many mentoring sessions together. I recall thinking, "How in the world can that be true? After all, it is called *sexual* addiction!"

That was nearly twenty years ago and my perspective has radically changed. Based on my own recovery journey and the privilege of helping addicts all over the world, I can attest that Page was precisely right. In fact, I recently ran across some of my notes and insights that date back to the years when he was helping me discover the underlying core-causes of my own sexual addiction. I referred to this earlier, but in this context it bears repeating:

> *During times of great stress and trauma, we all have our unique methods for escape and survival. Mine were withdrawal and isolation. I avoided confrontation at all costs. Rather than challenging my abusive stepfather, I submitted to him and tried to be invisible. I remember on many occasions curled up in the fetal position in my dark room, trembling and hoping my parents' raging on the other side of the wall didn't suddenly turn on me. I hated pressure and crumbled when I was put on the spot to perform: make the winning*

shot, speak in public, make a sales pitch, or even stand up for myself. I was so filled with anxiety, fear and self-doubt that I remember every morning of my 7th grade year arriving at school with horrible stomach cramps and racing straight to the restroom with diarrhea.

Then something happened that would change my life forever—I was introduced to pornography. I can remember the event like it was yesterday. A group of friends found a Playboy magazine. We all stood huddled around gawking at the images. I was overwhelmed, like I'd been struck by lightning. I had never felt a more powerful sensation. From that moment forward I was hooked. Living in the San Fernando Valley in southern California, the porn production capital of the world, I had no difficulty getting my hands on magazines. I had found my "drug of choice," a way to self-medicate and escape from the traumas of life. Finally, there was something that seemed to fill the hole in my soul. My self-preservation methods of withdrawal and isolation were a perfect match with pornography. Alone and in secret, I could disappear into a world of pleasure and fantasy—a world without pain, fear, violence or criticism.

We get BLHASTed

In my own addiction and with all my male clients, I have learned that we are most vulnerable to the temptations of pornography and other sexual behaviors when "something" isn't going right in our lives: marriage, children, work, health, finances, church, etc. Whenever we are feeling *BLHASTed*—**B**ored or **B**urned out, **L**onely, **L**ustful, **H**ungry, **A**ngry, **A**nxious or **A**fraid, **S**tressed or **T**ired, our brains have learned from long-tested and proven experience that sexual outlets are a powerful, accessible and reliable way to avoid, escape, cope, self-soothe and self-medicate. Entering the *Sexual Funnel* becomes our literal *drug of choice*.

But why do the brains of some individuals choose the Sexual Funnel as their coping strategy as opposed to a host of healthy alternatives? That is an extremely complex, multi-faceted question that could occupy an entire book. Remember that the brain's primary function and directive is to keep the body alive at all costs—*survival* is the brain's watchword. It is designed to be ever vigilant in scanning the environment, internal and external, for potential threats of any kind, real or imagined. Even a moderate discomfort, annoyance or concern can trigger the brain's warning system, evoking *emotions* (energy-in-motion) like those included in the acronym *BLHASTed*. True to its programming, the brain seeks for an immediate solution.

In the Brain, Addiction is *Hyper-Learning*

Imagine what happens in one of these intense emotional states, when the brain is searching for relief from one of a host of conditions, environments, influences or situations. Then it encounters the potent, pain-numbing, immediate stress-relieving chemical rush of the Sexual Funnel. The vigilant brain not only takes notice, it remembers and learns. In the future when discomfort, stress or dangers are again perceived, which option can easily appear at the top of the brain's remedy list?

Unfortunately, in our highly sexualized and technologically advanced society, the Sexual Funnel experience is instantly accessible. What starts out as an accidental exposure or unfortunate circumstance can quickly turn to purposely sought-after, repeated events, gradually becoming habit, morphing into compulsion and finally descending into the realm of addiction. The Sexual Funnel moves to the very top of the brain's solution list—the automatic go-to place when unwanted, painful emotions hit.

In the brain, addiction is *hyper-learning*. Once the brain links the Sexual Funnel as *the* remedy for discomfort, the problem and solution are literally *welded* together. It's not unlike *Pavlov's dogs*; stimulus and response. We know we've come to the place of full-fledged addiction when, in spite of negative consequences and the sacrifice of everyone and everything that truly matters to us, we continue to act out sexually. This brings us to a dark and hellish place of guilt, regret, self-loathing and shame. We are desperate to break free and inevitably the strategies we employ lead us to the perpetual trap of the *Avoidance Cycle* (which I will discuss in chapter 12).

USING SEX AS A MEANS TO COPE WITH TRAUMA

Stephen Moore

EARLY IN MY CAREER, I worked for the local District Attorney's Office as a Witness Assistant Intern with the Special Victims Unit. I was responsible for dealing with cases that involved domestic and sexual violence. I remember working with one client who had been through a serious physical assault; her injuries were clearly visible. This woman had been attacked by a domestic partner during an argument that had rapidly escalated out of control. She had a long road of physical recovery ahead of her.

As I met with her, it didn't take long to see that her emotional injuries ran even deeper than her physical trauma. She told me how she had been emotionally living in a place of fear, insecurity, desperation and very low self-esteem. This emotional wounding had been going on for years; the violence she had endured was a physical manifestation of the emotional abuse she had been through.

As I helped her prepare to testify against her attacker in court, we discussed many things: emotional regulation skills, mental exercises to use during difficult testimony, etc. I spent the most time talking with her about how to begin the healing journey toward lasting recovery. We talked about her nightmares; her fears of never being able to trust a man again; her struggle with feelings of deserving the emotional abuse she had endured.

Trauma is One-way Street

Of particular note in this example is that her abuser had made what appeared to be valiant attempts to make amends. He had written long letters and was being proactive in providing financial restitution. However sincere his efforts, they were of little help in this woman's internal and external healing. As much as he tried, this man was unable to take back what he had done to his former partner.

And so it is with anyone who has experienced emotional trauma. Forgiveness, reconciliation and amends—while very helpful to the healing process—*can't "un-traumatize" or heal a person*. Just as this victim's physical wounds had to heal on their own over time, she slowly realized that only she could do the work to find emotional healing and peace. All of us have endured some sort of emotional trauma. All of us have emotional wounds that need to heal. And even though those wounds may come from many different sources, the healing that must take place is an internal process. Friends, family, therapists and other forms of support can help, but *ultimately the individual must work toward healing.*

Emotional and Spiritual Trauma is in the Eye of the Beholder

I have come to realize that my own addiction originated from several factors, but the emotional trauma from my Dad's sudden death had the most impact. Following his plane crash, I was angry at everything and everyone. Though it caused me a lot of shame and guilt, I was angry at God—the unfairness of it all! The words of others did little to console me: "He must be needed on the other side." "Yeah, well, I needed him too!" I would internally cry out. I didn't care that there was a bigger (God's) plan at play. I didn't resonate with the idea that sometimes really bad things happen to good people through no fault of their own. None of these things mattered at the time. As a 12-year-old boy, all I knew was that my best friend had been taken from me, and that God had played some sort of role—or failed to.

Over time, this "spiritual trauma" continued to grow, in part because I ignored it and numbed out through my addiction. Like a festering wound that has become infected, these feelings of abandonment, anger and betrayal amplified and for a time, it seemed to cost me my testimony. I had been forced to conclude that either I was so "bad" that I didn't warrant the blessing of having a father around, or what I knew about God was actually wrong (which was partially true—more on this later).

Running From Our Wounds: Our Endless Attempt to Escape

Like too many others, my spiritual and emotional wounding is what kept me sick. It was the reason I struggled for nearly 20 years to put down the addiction. I wish I could say my story is unique, but since you are still reading it's likely that some parts of this story sound familiar. I felt abandoned. God had taken my Dad from me.

As addicts, we spend our lives lying, deceiving, cheating and manipulating. We have tried time and again to overcome our addictions, but despite our best efforts we have been unable to. While the addiction perpetuates a trap of shame, acting out, and disconnection, our behavior is only driven in part by lust. For most of us, lust has never been our end goal. We come to realize that our behaviors are an attempt to medicate, cope with, numb from, escape and avoid emotional and/or spiritual pain and trauma.

We often talk about our struggle as being "progressively addictive and destructive." This is certainly true, as all of us inevitably find out that one form of acting out is never enough. In order to continue escaping, we need more and more of our drug: more potent images, more graphic movies, different body types, different and novel forms of sexually acting out. While this is partially due to the progressive chemical and neurological need for more and more to maintain our "high," this is only a part of the equation. The other part is that our acting out—however enjoyable or effective it may be in the moment—never fills the void that emotional trauma and disconnection have left within us. We are trying to fill a gaping wound using cotton balls and bandages, when what we require is emotional surgery. *We use our addiction as a stop-gap measure*, a way to temporarily escape. Despite our best efforts, when our emotional and spiritual wounds are left untreated we will continue to emotionally "bleed out."

THE AVOIDANCE CYCLE: WHY TRYING HARDER DOESN'T WORK

Mark Kastleman

"**Y**OU JUST NEED to try harder!" "You just don't want it bad enough!" "What's wrong with your willpower?" "Just make up your mind and do it!" I've heard these statements, and dozens of variations, from other people and shouted them in my own mind at least a thousand times. The idea that sheer willpower and true grit can fix anything was ingrained in me by my familial, religious and societal cultures. I believed that my only hope for breaking free was to go to war with my unwanted sexual thoughts and urges.

What happens when you try to force a thought out of your mind? For instance, right now I don't want you to think about a big, bright, pink elephant. No matter what, DO NOT think about that elephant! Of course, the more you try to fight and keep the image out of your mind, the more it drills its way in. In psychology, this is called an *intrusive* thought. Continually attempting to fight and force the same intrusive sexual thoughts, urges or feelings out of your mind can hopelessly plunge you into the *Avoidance Cycle*.

The Avoidance Cycle

When we fight to overcome pornography use and other unwanted sexual behaviors, our go-to battle strategy is nearly always one of resistance, avoidance and sheer willpower.

For example, let's assume that an LDS man trying to overcome his addiction begins feeling the urge to look at pornography; he immediately goes to war with the thought, trying to force it out of his mind. He reasons, "I've got to avoid sexual thoughts at all costs." He grits his teeth, clenches his fists and uses sheer willpower to keep the thoughts and urges at bay.

As he attempts to force the sexual thoughts and urges out of his mind, they drill their way in with even more power, until they become intrusive. Often he fights long and hard, and then finally battle-worn and weary, he gives in and enters the Sexual Funnel.

As he views the images, powerful neurochemicals flood his brain and there is an immediate, highly satisfying relief from the battle. With a long exhale, he breathes the words, "Finally, I don't have to fight these sexual thoughts and urges anymore!" However, as he reaches the crescendo and then emerges from the narrow part of the Funnel, the neurochemicals dissipate, logic and reasoning return, followed by an almost instant flood of guilt, regret, confusion, frustration and shame. He pounds his fist declaring a new vow to fight the

THE AVOIDANCE CYCLE

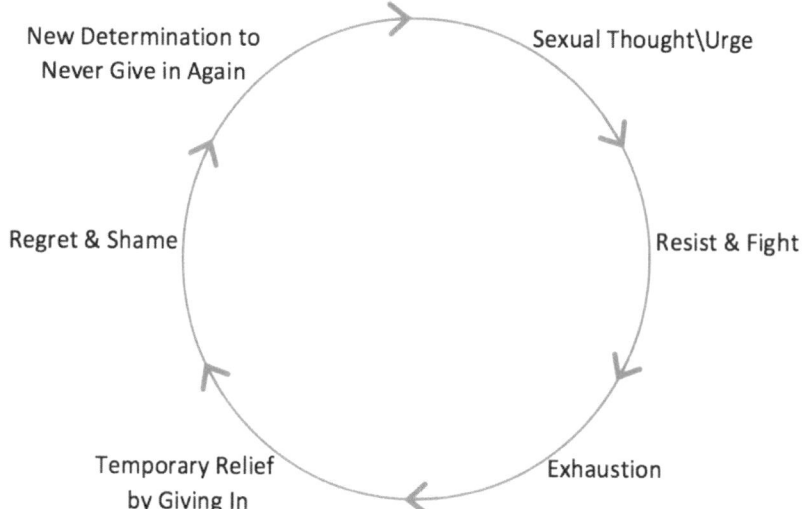

urge, and the whole *Avoidance Cycle* begins again—fighting, exhaustion, and giving in endlessly repeated.

Addicts can be hopelessly trapped in this cycle for years or even decades. "So," you might be thinking, "if avoidance and sheer willpower are not the answer, what is?" In the second half of this book, you will learn the answer to this question and the precise steps you must take to break out of the Avoidance Cycle. For now, let's explore the Avoidance Cycle from another angle.

The Control Phase

Another way to look at the Avoidance Cycle is in the form of two phases: the *Control Phase* and the *Release Phase*. First, let's look at the Control Phase by returning to the example of the LDS man who battles his urges until he's exhausted and gives in.

After emerging from the narrow part of the Sexual Funnel, his wide perspective restored, he can't believe he has fallen prey yet again to same urges! Feelings of guilt, regret, shame, frustration and hopelessness flood his mind. These dominant feelings can lead him to head right back into the Funnel for escape, or they can propel him into the *Control Phase*.

In the Control Phase, he declares, "I will never, ever do that again!" He is absolutely determined in his resolve. To make sure he succeeds, he moves into a state of *hyper-control*. He believes if he can be perfect—if he can completely control every thought and shut down every urge—he will finally be free. He believes others will finally accept him; he will finally accept himself; and at last he will be worthy and his shame and guilt will go away.

With determination, he grips the steering wheel of life even tighter and "white-knuckles" it through each day with gritted teeth. Just as he is excessive and extreme in his use of pornography, self-stimulation and other unwanted sexual behaviors, he is equally extreme in his quest to control everything and be perfect. Unfortunately, this perfection obsession often extends to his relationships with family, friends and colleagues. He clamps down on them as well as himself.

Being human, he can only keep this impossible pace of perfection up for so long until he is once again exhausted and stressed out of his mind. The Control Phase winds tighter and tighter until he has to find a release or his brain will explode! So, at the end of his rope, he leaves the Control Phase and enters the Release Phase.

The Release Phase

In the Release Phase, he gives in to his sexual thoughts and urges and acts out his unwanted behaviors. This gives him a temporary but tremendous release from the incredible stress and pressure of the Control Phase. After he escapes and self-medicates, all of the typical negative emotions and consequences hit him head on, and he resolves once again, "That was the last time!" and he moves right back into the Control Phase. The cycle between the Control and Release Phases has been called the "Rollercoaster Ride from Hell."

At times, he can exercise extreme willpower and stay in the Control Phase for weeks or even months. At other times, he can emerge from the Release Phase, make an attempt at control for a few hours, and then fall right back into unwanted behaviors. He can stay in the Release Phase escaping through sexual outlets for a few minutes, hours, days or even weeks.

It's important to note that many of the efforts he makes in the Control Phase aren't bad—many, in fact, can be good. The problem is, valiant efforts in the Control Phase focus on avoidance through sheer willpower, and in the brain willpower is a very limited, exhaustible and often fickle resource.

Willpower Depletion

We found that as people depleted their willpower, they became increasingly likely to give in to desires they might otherwise have resisted. That remarkable statement was offered in an interview with renowned researcher and social psychologist, Dr. Roy Baumeister. He and his colleagues at Florida State University have spent decades studying willpower and decision-making in human beings.

Have you ever thought of willpower as a finite resource, a reservoir that can be drained and depleted? Extensive brain and behavioral studies have clearly shown that people perform poorly on self-control tests when they have engaged in earlier acts of willpower and self-control in seemingly unrelated activities. For example, in one study Baumeister's team invited a group of test subjects to freely eat freshly baked chocolate-chip cookies, while asking a second group to resist the cookies and munch on radishes instead. Then the team gave both groups impossible geometry puzzles to solve. Those who freely ate the cookies had sufficient willpower to work on the puzzles an average of 20 minutes, while the cookie-resisting group gave up after only 8 minutes.

Think of the brain as having a kind of *willpower fuel tank*. Research shows that on average, we spend in total some 3-4 hours a day resisting a wide variety of urges and desires. On top of that, willpower is used for many other things like controlling thoughts and emotions, regulating tasks and making decisions.

Keep in mind that in addition to managing all of the regular activities, responsibilities, stresses and pressures of daily life, the sexual addict also expends enormous amounts of willpower resisting a continual bombardment of sexual thoughts, images, cues and triggers. Throughout the course of the day, all of this drains his willpower fuel tank. If sheer willpower and *trying harder* is his primary resistance strategy, how successful will he be after a particularly stressful day when a tidal wave of sexual temptation hits him head on?

Sheer willpower is not enough and is not the answer to breaking free from pornography use, masturbation and other unwanted sexual behaviors. You will learn there is a much better way!

HOW YOU'RE FIGHTING IS PART OF THE PROBLEM

Stephen Moore

IN THE MOVIE "Saving Private Ryan," there is a scene I often use with clients. During World War II, a German soldier is captured by Allied forces. Through desperate attempts to gain favor, the captive earns the trust of an Allied commander in the platoon that captured him, and the commander eventually frees the German. Within a matter of days, the same Allied commander is ambushed by a group of German soldiers, including his former captive.

The following scene is a powerful one: while the Allied commander tries to find cover, the German soldier he recently released aims his rifle at his former captor, looks him straight in the face and shoots him without hesitation. The men that view this clip find it difficult not to feel a mix of frustration and betrayal; how could this former prisoner shoot the very man who freed him? How heartless he must be! By contrast, other clients find the Allied commander to be at fault; he had his enemy at his mercy, and allowed him to go free.

This provides an interesting parallel for how we approach our recovery from addiction. Let me ask you a very direct question: *Is your addiction your enemy?* Many of us immediately answer, "Of course it is!" To those who answer this way in my groups, I almost immediately challenge their response. "Is your addiction truly your enemy, or has it somehow become your friend? Are there ways you sympathize with it? Nurture it? Use it as a scapegoat?" This is a common example of the extremely delusional thinking most of us slip into while caught up in our addiction. This should come as no surprise. As poisonous as our addiction is, as much as it's killing us and robbing us of everything we hold dear, we too often give it a place to stay and continue on. Sure, we may kick it out of the living room on occasion and feel pride for making that decision. While this is a good step, is it really enough? If you removed an intruder from your home, but allowed him to steal the car from your garage, did that solve your problem? Would that make sense?! This logic sounds ridiculous to most people, but it's a common rationale for one who has grown dependent on his addiction. He desires freedom from it, but doesn't know how to live without it.

Know the Face of Your Enemy

Do we blame the German for mercilessly gunning down the commander who released him? Is he evil, or have we overlooked his nature? I believe the commander failed to remember that his enemy's job was to escape and keep fighting at any cost. Friends, if you are going to effectively fight this addiction, you must see the face of your enemy for what it really is. Your addiction is not your friend. It is not your buddy, pal or chum. Though it masks itself as having your best interests at heart, it cares nothing for your well-being or lasting happiness.

Like our German soldier, your addiction will do anything to stay alive. That is its nature. It will lie to you. Your addiction is like a voracious predator that can never be satisfied. It's a wild animal that doesn't recognize your desire or right to live free. It will take everything, and give nothing in return. It doesn't care about how the decision to act out now will leave you feeling 5 minutes, 30 minutes, or days after the fact; it only cares about *feeling good* here and now—the high; the Escape. You've been duped into trading dollars for dimes, and have been convinced that you are getting a steal of a deal, when you're actually being robbed blind. In 12-Step programs all over the world, a popular phrase is used: "Half measures availed us nothing." When it comes to recovery from sexual addiction, truer words have never been spoken.

We Set Ourselves Up for Failure

"I just need to try harder next time." It's not an exaggeration to say that if addicts had a dollar for each time we think or utter this phrase, we would be well off. I've observed addicts trying to tap into true grit to get the job done, and watched well-meaning men say they'll try harder, even as the tone of their voice betrays them. Will "trying harder" really work? Has it worked for you up to this point? If you're still reading, chances are it hasn't. It's time for some straight talk: you don't need to try *harder*; you need to try *smarter*.

When we lack the knowledge or support to adequately fight our addiction, we're like the man who brings a knife to a gunfight. Each time we try harder, we tell ourselves "maybe if I bring a bigger knife," or "maybe if I bring more knives." You don't need a bigger knife, my friend; you need some heavy artillery. Battling this addiction may be the hardest thing you will ever do, and if you want to win the war, you've got to start thinking outside the box.

White Knuckling: the Enemy of Lasting Recovery

"I just need to say, 'no'." We have all tried this route, and most of us haven't found what we are looking for. "White knuckling," or relying on one's own willpower to overcome addiction, is perhaps the biggest mistake I see clients make. It was also my biggest stumbling block to lasting recovery.

Willpower will never be enough. We are addicts because our willpower, at least around our addiction, is severely compromised. We have a hole in our armor: an affinity for sexually acting out. If we're to find real recovery, we must remember that we are more vulnerable to that place of fantasy and lust than the average person. Though it's something I don't consciously think about anymore, in the early days of my recovery I had to be mindful of every possible trigger. Our addiction can play off anything. I once worked with a heroin addict who also struggled with sexual addiction. He told me, "Having a sex addiction is like walking around with my heroin dealer in my pocket all the time." And he's right. To act out in our sexual addiction—to go to that place of fantasy, escape, or numbing out—we don't need anything more than our own minds.

The sad reality is that our past history with sexual addiction has trained our minds to be able to recall, and even create, sexually charged material. In the past there was a part of my mind that could create more pornographic images and situations than I could ever find online. I had a porn film set, with a camera crew at the ready, in my brain. I have often found the same dynamic with my clients. These days, I am grateful to say that the camera set is covered in sheets and a thick layer of dust, neglected and forgotten. While I say this gratefully, I also do so realizing that if I don't remain on guard, the stage could easily be dusted off and put back into action.

Depending solely on our willpower to save us is like lowering a bucket into a dry well and expecting it to bring up water: no matter how much you wish for it, the empty bucket doesn't deliver. We have to rally other resources to effectively tackle this monster in our lives. White knuckling is helpful and necessary in the recovery process, but it's not much more than a stop-gap measure. It will work in a pinch, but it's unreliable and short-lived. A wide range of recovery tools can help you avoid falling back into old patterns. For example, reaching out to others in your support system can help you identify faulty thinking. You can't do it alone. And that's okay. *You were never meant to.*

"GOD AND I CAN HANDLE THIS JUST FINE" ... REALLY?

Mark Kastleman

I HAVE OFTEN lamented that nearly all LDS men (and most men in general) fear discovery of their sexual addiction behaviors more than they fear death. This was certainly the case for me. We are absolutely convinced that revealing our dark secret will have a cataclysmic impact on our most cherished relationships (spouse, children, grandchildren, friends, work, church, neighbors). We believe it will obliterate our image, our reputation and forever alter the way others see and interact with us, branding us with the permanent label of *pervert*. We fear disclosure will destroy our lives.

This intense fear can drive us into *stealth mode,* where we go to elaborate and even outrageous lengths to keep our behaviors hidden: covert internet and social media accounts; an undisclosed cell phone; clandestine credit cards and payment methods; traveling great distances to avoid people we know; orchestrating times and situations when we can be alone and isolated. We can put up emotional decoys, create intricate excuses and generate clever distractions if someone gets too suspicious or close to discovery. This masquerade becomes mentally, emotionally and spiritually draining, and can consume ever-increasing amounts of time and resources. In some ways, this secrecy is more destructive to our relationships with self, others and God than the addiction itself.

God and I Can Handle This

Because we are consumed by the fear of discovery, we begin to concoct all kinds of rationalizations and justifications designed to talk ourselves out of disclosure and getting help. One of the most common rationalizations I used for decades, one implemented at some time or another by most men is: *God and I can handle this just fine; no one else needs to know.*

Of course this is in direct conflict with the clearly established fundamental principle of *confessing all of our serious sins to a bishop or stake president.* That choice is unthinkable because we are certain that it will bring all of our worst fears to fruition. "No," we silently calculate, "there must be another way." With a little convenient massaging of scripture and the creative interpretation of doctrine, we find what we perceive to be a way to stay hidden while still complying with God's will. Here's some of our reasoning:

> Can't I confess my sins directly to the Lord? Have I not been directed to seek a close and personal relationship with Heavenly Father? Should I not counsel with Him in all my doings? Didn't Christ suffer for all of my sins and can't I obtain forgiveness through Him? Alma the Younger received forgiveness in a coma without confessing to anyone but God! If I confess directly to God and then show my true sincerity and repentance by never giving in to sexual temptations again, then I have repented, right? Doesn't God have all power to help me, far more than a mortal man? I really think God and I can handle this on our own. No one else needs to be involved.

We may conjure up sufficient courage to disclose *some* of our sexual behaviors while diminishing, understating or hiding altogether the more serious indulgences. We reason that while others may tolerate the confession of minor or even moderate mistakes, they could never love or accept us after learning about our serious offenses!

Having creatively maneuvered our way into this realm of reasoning and rationalization, we breathe a sigh of relief, grateful that we can keep up our outward appearance of propriety and perfection while working with God on our most serious, unwanted sexual behaviors. And so, (as you learned in chapter 12) we privately confess to God another relapse, pound our fist on the table declaring, "That's the last time!" and move back into the *Control Phase* as we have hundreds of times before.

Dominated by our fears, we don't realize that a wise and loving Heavenly Father did not give us the principle of confession as a cruel device for exposure and shame, but rather as a divine gift that opens the door to love, understanding, support, brotherhood, peace and eventual freedom. As you will learn repeatedly in this book, the opposite of addiction is not sobriety; it is *connection.* And one of the most intimate acts of connection is full and sacred confession to another human being.

How Did You Find Out?

It seems there is a pandemic of secrecy, fear and shame among LDS men hopelessly struggling with pornography and other sexual addiction behaviors. So many desperately need help and yet relatively few are willing to take the risk of full disclosure. As addicts in disguise sitting in elders quorums and high priests groups, they feel uniquely flawed, weak and wicked. Yet all around them are men with similar struggles equally afraid to open up and get the help they need. A close friend of mine shares his first courageous attempt at divulging his struggles and just how fearful our LDS culture can be:

> *I was super active in my ward and had served in a lot of important positions. It was a pretty closely-knit LDS community and we all knew each other really well. It seemed like we were constantly at the ward building for activities, dances, dinners, sports, fireworks and everything in between. I thought of myself as well respected and well liked. I went to great lengths to dress in the right Sunday attire, to talk the right Mormon lingo, to give awesome Sacrament meeting talks and class lessons. I always volunteered for the service opportunities and was the first to show up and the last to leave. For me, my*

image as a priesthood holder and measuring up in the eyes of the members and leaders was a top priority.

The problem was, the whole time I was nothing but a big hypocrite because I was completely hooked on porn, masturbation and some other related behaviors. I just battled it out on my own for years, petrified of anyone ever finding out, including and especially my wife. Finally the whole trying and failing cycle got so miserable and depressing and hopeless that I knew I had to get some help. So I decided that I would tell my bishop who was also a good friend—which made it even more terrifying! I was so embarrassed and awkward about it I couldn't just make an appointment and go in. I had to create some roundabout way to do it.

I had a book on addiction and one of the chapters was about sexual addiction. I had highlighted in yellow all of the sections of the chapter that described my struggles and actions. I walked up to the bishop and said simply, "Would you read the highlighted parts of this chapter and then call me so we can get together?" With that I quickly walked away almost hyperventilating!

Weeks went by and I didn't hear from him. I started to panic as I thought, "I knew it! He read the chapter and saw all the marked sections and now he knows everything and is totally disgusted with me!" My mind started creating all kinds of disaster scenarios—excommunication, divorce, a ruined reputation. Then a few days later he called to set up a time to meet. Anticipating that meeting was pure torture!

The time came and as I walked through his door I saw him with his head in his hands and the book sitting on his desk. He looked totally depressed and dejected and I thought, "I knew it, I'm dead meat!" I sat down and as he lifted up his head to look at me he quietly asked, "How did you find out?" Confused, I responded, "How did I find out what?" Then he explained, "When you gave me the book and I read the highlighted sections, my heart sank. Everything you marked were the very struggles I faced during my own addiction years. How in the world did you find out about my past?"

To say I was stunned would be a gross understatement. My dropping jaw must have hit the floor. There was what seemed like an eternity of silence and then I quietly said, "I didn't give you the book because of your past, I gave it to you so you could read all about the addiction I'm caught up in right now. It's not about you, it's about me."

Well, for a minute we just sat there and looked at each other and then kind of spontaneously we both let out a gasp and a nervous laugh. What a crazy situation and what a sad commentary on the fear and shame we both felt as LDS men. That experience changed my life and finally got me out of my secrecy and isolation and to the help I needed. It still took several years to get a handle on my addiction, but for the first time in my life I wasn't going it alone, and that made all the difference!

THE DOCTOR WILL SEE YOU NOW, BUT ARE YOU WILLING TO SEE HIM?

Stephen Moore

SOME YEARS AGO, I went to the doctor for a routine physical exam. Having had cancer twice consecutively as a child, I go in once a year to have a general physical with a few fairly routine blood tests. My wife and I were out and about that day; stopping at the doctor's office was just one of many things planned. I felt like I was in good health, and figured this visit would go like many others I'd had for nearly 20 years since my cancer was beaten into long-term remission. I thought the staff would run a few tests, the doctor would come in and give the usual rundown of results, and I would be on my way.

The first half of the visit went exactly as I anticipated: small talk with the doctor, some joking around, but when he returned that quickly changed. I learned a "normal range" for this particular test was between 80 and 120 mg/dL of blood, but my blood sugar level was nearly 500 mg/dL. The doctor said someone with a level that high would typically be in a coma, yet I felt fine. He then explained that it had likely been that high for some time, and that because I had built up a "tolerance" to such high levels, I felt "normal" even though I was far from it.

The unexpected diagnosis of diabetes stunned and scared me. I was angry at my body for letting me down and angry at God for letting my body fail me. Just as I had felt following my Dad's death years before, this was another manifestation of how God must not care about me or my happiness. Cancer twice; a fatherless childhood. Hadn't I been through enough?

I immediately called my Mom to tell her. I tried to remain calm, but I began crying (mothers often have the ability to cut through one's armor that way). I remember telling her how frustrated I was, and then I said, "Mom, I just want to be normal." I didn't want to be "weak" or "broken."

Have you ever felt this way, specifically with regard to your addiction? Those who are partners and family members of addicts have likely felt this way about their relationship and/or marriage with an addicted family member. Most addicts have uttered such sentiments many times: sometimes when leaning on loved ones and other times on their knees, in desperation and through choked sobbing. I have had many such conversations with myself, with my wife, and with God. "Why do I have to go through this? I didn't ask for this! I don't want any part of it anymore! *I just want to be normal.*"

Denial is Part of What Keeps You Sick

Although I learned definitively that summer day about my diabetes diagnosis, the sad truth is that I remained in denial about it. I made a few changes but minimized its significance. "Surely it isn't as bad as they said," I would tell myself. I made a few half-hearted efforts to change initially, but didn't stick to them. The longer I remained in denial, the more the evidence surfaced that I really was sick. But just as we do in our addictions, I blew off, rationalized and justified both my choices and their consequences. This went on for some time, until I began to experience some bigger warning signs. It was only when these danger signals hit a certain threshold that I began to make serious change.

How many times have you done what I did? How many little bits of evidence that something is terribly wrong have you ignored or justified? How many metaphorical "stop signs" have you run through, often at full speed? These warnings might include an ultimatum from a spouse, separation and/or divorce or legal consequences. They scream a reality that each of us must finally admit: I am addicted, and I cannot stop. Generally speaking, most of us don't arrive at this place on our own.

Unfortunately at this point, pain and life experience become our teachers. As the consequences of our actions mount and our addiction grows, *we are eventually forced to a crossroads: we have to make a choice.* We can choose our addiction and everything that comes with it, or we can seek recovery and all of its benefits, *but we cannot have both.* While this is often a painful and challenging process, I can tell you that it's also a tremendous blessing. This is the point where we can begin living—really living—for the first time in a long time, or for some of us, for the very first time.

Things Are Not Always What They Seem

I don't like to wear glasses. I didn't always need them. As a kid I had 19/20 vision, which is actually better than "perfect" 20/20 vision. I thought I had dodged a genetic bullet: both of my parents began wearing glasses early in their lives, and until a few years ago I was optimistic that I would never need them. But life has a way of throwing us curve balls and I began to realize my vision was slowly changing. At first small signs in the distance became difficult to read. Within a year I needed glasses, particularly for night vision. After a long day, my eyes were tired and the blurriness would get worse after dark.

Before I purchased the glasses, I wasn't aware of just how bad my vision had become. During the year prior, I had grown accustomed to squinting at things in the distance and not reading signs until I was close to them. My vision wasn't so bad that I couldn't function, but it made a lot of things difficult and my quality of life was diminished.

Even when it became obvious that I needed glasses, I resisted because I didn't want to spend the money. "What a waste!" I told myself. Surely that money could be spent on something more satisfying. The day I finally bought my glasses, I was frustrated and still in denial. But when I put them on, it was shocking to realize how bad my vision really was. Suddenly I remembered what it was like to see things in focus. *My sight had deteriorated so gradually*, I had actually forgotten what it was like to see clearly. The experience was an emotional one; I had regained something I hadn't even realized was gone.

Like vision that deteriorates slowly, our addiction to lust, sex and fantasy happens slowly over time. Often the change is so subtle, so slight, that the difference isn't perceptible. When clients first come to work with me, they typically are still on the fence with their addiction; they want to be done with it, but question whether the cost is worth it. At the beginning of recovery, trusting your therapist, sponsor and others that can see your situation clearly is critical.

Correcting Your Vision Takes Time

We typically "buy in" to the recovery process over time, and an important benchmark occurs when we begin to get our metaphorical vision back. Looking through the "glasses" of recovery, we start to see our lives and the world around us more clearly. We see that our previous version of reality was a lie. Addiction slowly blurred our thinking, particularly regarding shame (that we are beyond recovery or hope) and denial (that our problems are smaller than they actually are). These early glimpses of recovery take many forms: the marriage that starts to heal, less anger and resentment towards self and others, longer periods of sobriety. These experiences help solidify our commitment to recovery. We not only see the need to recover for others, we desire it for ourselves and we have experiences that tell us it may be possible.

I Will Get Support, Once I Have a Handle on It

"Two weeks," I would tell myself. "That's how long I need to be free of my behavior before I go tell the bishop, or talk to a therapist about it. Once I have a handle on it, then I can talk about it, confess and really move forward." It's interesting to (gratefully) be in a stage of long-term recovery and to see how deluded this sentiment looks to me now, even as I recall how much this made sense in my addicted brain at the time. There were many flaws in my thinking then, but perhaps the most egregious were: 1) a complete misunderstanding of addiction and how it works; 2) denial about the fact that I was out of control, and couldn't stop my ever-deepening addictive behavior, and 3) my desire to avoid the consequences of my actions.

At the time, I looked at the whole "talk to your priesthood leader" concept as a process where you confessed and absolved transgression. In my teenage mind, the bishop could tell me I was "good to go"— the person whose stamp of approval I needed to move forward in my priesthood responsibilities, going on a mission, etc. A part of me was convinced that if talked to him while still active in my addiction, I would face increasingly serious church discipline, so it was easier to keep it a secret. I always took pride in not lying to my priesthood leaders about my addiction; if cornered and asked point-blank how I was doing, I was honest about it. However, I would avoid these conversations at all costs. I recall seeing the bishop in the hallway more than once while at church, and ducking into the restroom or turning the other way to avoid him.

I was minimizing the significance of my problem, and I was convinced that he couldn't really help me. "Everyone I've told before this hasn't been able to help me, so why bother?" This was partially true; the bishops I had worked with knew little about addiction or the depth of my issue, and had given me advice that never produced lasting change despite my best efforts to follow it. However, had I been more forthcoming, chances are a bishop could have led me to a qualified therapist—someone I may have been willing to listen to. That conversation may have radically changed my addiction and recovery path. But just as I avoided full candor with the bishop, I had the same problem with therapy when I first began attending. I went erratically a few times over the years prior to getting into recovery, but inevitably would simply quit going. In the end, I didn't want to talk about it because, like my diabetes diagnosis, acknowledging it made it more real; something I had to face.

Talking with my clients about my old way of thinking inevitably hits a nerve and they resonate with much of it. This is a common thread among addicts. *We convince ourselves that going to the doctor will be helpful, but only after we have recovered from our illness*! It's important to ask yourself the same question I was forced to ask: does this way of thinking make any sense? If you had cancer, would you put off seeing the doctor until it went away? Of course not.

You don't need to reinvent the wheel. When you finally face the reality that something has to change, you have two choices: you can fully accept the seriousness of your situation and tackle your addiction, or pain and consequences will drive you to that point. As someone who has gone down both roads, I would advise you to choose the former.

THE MORE YOU DRINK SALT WATER, THE MORE YOU THIRST

Stephen Moore

WHEN I WAS YOUNG, I spent a lot of time at my grandparents' home in Orem, Utah, and have many fond memories there: family reunions, water balloon volleyball in the backyard, racing "boats" (they were really just sticks) with my cousins in the small ditch running through the back of their property, and countless family and holiday gatherings.

After family meals, one of my favorite activities was taking the leftover corncobs and watermelon rinds to feed the horses in the pasture. As my cousins and I carried these scraps, it was as if the horses could sense that "treats" were coming. They would gather from all over the pasture to the fence for a feeding frenzy. It was a great opportunity to experience the horses up close, which I loved to do.

Unfortunately, I found that I am highly allergic to them. Being close to horses doesn't do much to me, but if I make physical contact with them and then touch my face, my eyes begin to run and my nose quickly becomes congested. As a kid I would touch my face and eyes all the time after feeding the horses. I learned that when I would scratch my face or rub my eyes to relieve the itching, it would relieve the symptoms for a short time, but the momentary relief created a greater desire to itch and scratch again.

Feeding the horses was always enjoyable, but inevitably I ended up having to go wash my hands, eyes and face thoroughly so I could keep my allergic reaction from escalating. Even after that, it would often take time for the symptoms to subside.

Allergic to Lust

As addicts, we are allergic to lust. We simply cannot tolerate it in any form; when we encounter it, we are inevitably affected by it in some way. Often this "allergic reaction" is puzzling to others and frustrating to us; we struggle with denial about the significance of our allergy. Like my stubborn younger self who was unwilling to keep a safe distance from my grandfather's horses, we often minimize or justify the consequences of exposure to lust, and we do it in many different ways.

"Secrets keep us sick" is a phrase often used in 12-Step programs, and for good reason. It's easy to understand this saying through the lens of keeping secrets from other people, but we do the same with ourselves. Just as I was unique among my cousins in my allergy to the horses, so we are unique in our allergy to lust. There are simply some situations and circumstances that we cannot tolerate; situations that others (to our chagrin) seemingly can. Whether it's a favorite TV show or movie, or a habit like staying up late that leaves us vulnerable, the truth is when we engage with lust, we pay a price. It changes our behavior and our thinking. The more we associate with our "allergy" the more severe the reaction becomes. These reactions are cumulative, and increase along with our exposure to lust. The longer we dance with the devil, the more of an influence it has over us.

"Maybe I'm Cured." Then Again, Maybe Not

Addicts find clever ways to justify engaging with our "allergy." I distinctly remember telling myself all sorts of half-truths during my active addiction to justify engaging with my drug. Some time ago, I was running a group therapy session. All of the group members were men struggling with sexual compulsivity; all were in early recovery. One client I'll call Jack walked into group, and I immediately began picking up on signs of shame from him. He wouldn't make eye contact with me and was less engaged than normal. While "checking in" with the group, he disclosed that he had relapsed in his addiction. This was somewhat surprising, as Jack was typically a group leader, had been active in completing assignments and participation, and had completed a significant length of sobriety.

When I asked him why he thought he had relapsed, he gave an answer that might sound insane to someone with no history of sexual addiction. "I've been doing so well that I wondered if maybe I was 'cured.' It sounds crazy, but I've been feeling so much less lust lately, I thought it would be a good idea to 'test my recovery' to see if I was really strong enough." He had deliberately exposed himself to a lust trigger to see if he was still allergic. This type of mental gamesmanship is all too common in our addict mindset; our brains play all sorts of tricks to justify another "hit" of our sexual drug. Just as I kept interacting with my grandfather's horses, each time expecting that I would be free of my allergy, we are often led to a place of unrealistic expectation on our path to recovery. We see progress and mistake it for victory.

Mark covered the brain science behind some of what we are discussing earlier, but simply put, the part of your brain where addiction lives doesn't care about consequences. How you will feel five minutes, an hour, or a day after acting out doesn't register with this part of the brain. All an addicted brain cares about is *feeling good—now, in this moment, regardless of the consequences.* The first component of real recovery isn't sobriety; *it is coming to accept your faulty thinking for what it is.* This involves an ongoing process of breaking through denial and gaining a better understanding of the enemy within.

The More You Drink, the More You Thirst

Several years ago my wife and I learned to snorkel. One of the first things we learned was to be very careful about not drinking too much saltwater. At first this sounded confusing: our bodies are mostly comprised of water. But drinking from the ocean doesn't hydrate the body. Drinking salt water can momentarily feel like it quenches your thirst, but the more you drink, the more you become *dehydrated.*

Lust works exactly the same way; as addicts, all of us have been there haven't we? We give in to our "thirst" for a lot of different reasons. We tell ourselves, "This is it, after tonight, I'm going to get serious about this," or "Just a little bit won't hurt; this is much less harmful than what I used to do." Each time we dupe ourselves into thinking that a little indulgence will bring relief from whatever we want to avoid (thoughts, feelings, shame), the further we remove ourselves from what we really want (deep connection). A powerful quote from Sexaholics Anonymous describes this dilemma:

"The only way we knew how to be free of it was to do it ... Conning ourselves time and again that the next one would save us, we were really losing our lives." (SA White Book, "The Problem," 2002 edition)

My history of battling addiction and helping clients do the same has taught me this truth: *no form of acting out in your addiction will ever be enough.* There will never be a piece of pornography, a sexual encounter or sexual fantasy that will quench your thirst. You will always walk away after drinking from the ocean of lust with a thirst for more. One of my favorite quotes is spoken by John Candy in the movie, "Cool Runnings:" *"If you're not enough without it, you'll never be enough with it."*

Are you ready to quench the thirst? Do you want to find genuine emotional, spiritual and sexual fulfillment? Read on! We will show you how.

SEXUAL ADDICTION IS AN *INTIMACY DISORDER*

Mark Kastleman

T***hrough my teen years*** and much of my adult life, I was hyper-vigilant to project an outward appearance that I believed was essential for others to respect and accept me. My greatest fear was that people would somehow discover the truth about my innumerable sins (especially the sexual ones), weaknesses, flaws, fears and inadequacies—my *dark side*. I was absolutely certain that if I ever discarded the mask and let down my guard to reveal the raw and real me, my life would never be the same. Knowing the full truth, people close to me would never see me the same again. Perhaps not openly, but certainly in their hearts and minds, they would judge, despise and reject me. The risk of disclosure was unthinkable and so my elaborate game of charades spanned many decades.

I recall being surprised in my early years of work with men struggling with sexual addiction. It was like looking in a mirror: every one of them wore masks, and this was especially true among my LDS clients. We care deeply about how we are perceived. Do we measure up as priesthood holders? Are we seen as being among the worthy, obedient, faithful, spiritual, knowledgeable and charitable? Do we give impressive talks and lessons, respond with intelligent comments in class, give enough service or hold the right callings? It's like we're constantly battling to fill a respect-acceptance-worthiness hole in our souls that never seems satisfied. Why? Because we have an innate, eternal need for *intimacy* and we go searching for it in all the wrong places.

Exhausted by the endless effort to measure up and maintain appearances, some men simply give up and leave the church. But many strive to keep up this outward-appearance/church-centered approach for a lifetime. Day after day we carry on the facade, terrified of what will happen if we ever allow others to penetrate our fortress walls and discover the dark secrets that lie hidden within. We pretend to have deep, honest, transparent relationships, and at times may even believe we do, but in reality we only allow people to see the surface. When it comes to our deep, dark struggles we are convinced that the only solution is secrecy and going it alone. As one of my clients put it, "I was going to take my sexual addiction secrets to the grave and let God sort them out later."

Saved by Grace After All We Can Do

There is one small window of hope that sex addicts often conjure up in their minds: "If I can somehow manage to conquer this addiction and get an extended period of sobriety and worthiness, then I can be honest and open and finally God and people will love and accept me." Sadly, they often use a well-known, consistently quoted scripture in 2 Nephi to justify this strategy: . . . *"for we know that it is by grace that we are saved, after all that we can do."*

This brief declaration and its *misinterpretation* among LDS men who struggle with addiction, has created a great deal of shame, hopelessness and *going it alone*. For decades I believed, "God will only help me after I've done ALL I can do on my own. And ALL I can do is to overcome these despicable sexual behaviors. Once I do that, then grace will kick in."

This belief was certainly not unique to me. I have encountered it in the hearts and minds of nearly every LDS client I've ever worked with. Years ago, the following visual came into my mind while I was pondering on this conundrum of independent action and effort vs. grace:

> *After a nearly constant lifelong battle and desperate struggle with sexual urges, temptations and addiction, I finally arrive near my mortal finish line—bruised, bloody, broken and spent. To cover the last few yards, I literally crawl on my belly, clawing with my torn fingernails to inch my emaciated body forward. With my last gasping breath, I manage to barely touch the edge of the chalked finish line. Only then, Jesus who is standing on the other side reaches down and lifts me up. Saved by grace after ALL I can do!*

You may be thinking, "How is it possible that an active priesthood holder, a returned missionary raised in the church, serving in myriad callings, intensely studying and teaching the gospel—how could he buy into such an extreme view of works vs. grace?"

The Distortion of Shame

Somewhere along the way, we develop a deep and malignant sense of unworthiness, brokenness, weakness, isolation, self-loathing and self-hatred—all hallmarks of the insidious feeling of *shame*. More than just a feeling, shame becomes an *identity*. I haven't simply made mistakes; I *am* a mistake.

As you learned in chapter 5, shame drives us *outside Christ's circle* and we are convinced that the only solution is to *earn* our way back in through independent effort and success in overcoming our unwanted sexual behaviors. *If* we can manage through sheer grit and monumental acts of will to attain sobriety for a long time, *then* we will be welcomed back into Christ's circle and enjoy the grace that all the other "non-addict" Latter-day Saints are privileged to receive.

This mindset of massive independent effort rewarded with a few drops of grace is a filter through which we interpret our overall gospel experience; our relationship and interactions with our Father, our Savior, those around us and ourselves. We cannot see, let alone comprehend, the *fallacy of the independent man*. We have no way of knowing that this *go it alone* and *earn grace* approach to life is at the very heart of why we remain trapped. The opposite of addiction is *connection*; addiction is an *intimacy disorder.*

Intimacy is Our True and Natural Condition

If you were to ask the average person on the street, "What's the first thing you think of when you hear the word intimacy?" many would respond with the word "sex." I've tested this theory with hundreds of audiences across America and it's true. If it's an all-male audience, this response is nearly unanimous. Yet intimacy is so much more than just physical. In fact, two people can come together sexually and not be intimate. Sexual intimacy is just one very small piece of the grand and beautiful intimacy landscape.

The simplest way I know to understand intimacy in its truest form is through hyphenating the word itself: *in-to-me-you-see.* True intimacy is manifest in the courageous, vulnerable act of allowing others to see us at our raw and real core, without walls, masks, facades, charades or pretense. In-to-me-you-see with all of my sins, flaws, darkness, weakness and foolishness; and my strengths, innate goodness, beauty, light, righteous desires and amazingness! With true intimacy, what you see is what you get—how liberating!

The fact is, true intimacy is what we crave; it's what we must have in order to be healthy, happy and fulfilled. Why? Because true intimacy is our natural condition; it's who we are at our eternal core. Before we were thrust down to this fallen world and into these fallen bodies, we came from a wondrous eternal world of complete transparency, openness, honesty, unconditional love and acceptance. As Eternal Beings in our heavenly home, we could simply be our real and raw selves, freely expressing thoughts, feelings, opinions, strengths and weaknesses.

True intimacy IS our natural state; we long for it and must have it to feel safe, fulfilled and joyful; to be physically, emotionally and spiritually healthy. Yet, we fear that which we most need. *I want to reveal my true, innermost self to you but I'm scared to death that when you find out who I really am you will reject me!* So we seek to fill our natural need for intimacy in ways we perceive to be free from the risks of transparency and vulnerability.

Our Savior practiced true intimacy all the days of His mortal ministry, and He yearned for each of us to reclaim this precious gift. It was a central focus of His intercessory prayer in John, chapter 17. Within three verses (21-23) he pleads for this intimacy three times: "*That they all may be one; as thou, Father, art in me, and I in thee, that they also may be one in us; that they may be one, even as we are one; I in them, and thou in me, that they may be made perfect in one.*"

Out of Fear, the Fallen Brain Seeks a Counterfeit Intimacy

While our eternal souls are at home with true intimacy, our fallen brains convince us that the risk is too great because it involves uncertainty and emotional exposure. Vulnerability is too high a price to pay for the connection we so desperately need. Perhaps somewhere along the way we risked intimacy and were hurt, rejected, let down or abused, and from then on the brain retreated into a self-protection mode. Yet the longing is still there, so we settle for cheap imitations of intimacy that give the temporary sensation of connection without the perceived risks. These connection substitutes often involve outlets that can quickly become addictive like alcohol, drugs, gambling, gaming, food, pornography and other sexual outlets.

Imagine a man who desperately needs real, intimate connections in his life. He may be completely numbed to this need. He may have been raised in a family environment where he didn't learn how to be intimate. He may be too afraid to take the risk. Regardless of the reasons, the unmet need expands, creating an intimacy void or *hole in the soul.*

Then, through an endless array of possible scenarios in our sexualized culture, he is exposed to pornography and other sexual outlets and makes the mistake of indulging. He enters the *Sexual Funnel* where a tidal wave of powerful neurochemicals are released, giving his brain and body a rush that *feels* like an intimate connection and temporarily appears to fill the void. This *counterfeit* can quickly evolve into his go-to place whenever he feels disconnected and empty.

Of course, fantasy can never take the place of true intimacy. Each indulgence leaves him more isolated and empty than before, and his mortal fear of being discovered pushes him deeper into secrecy and farther away from the authentic connection he so desperately needs. He feels hopelessly trapped in a downward spiral that never stops.

There is Great Hope!

The first section of this book describes how and why LDS men can become trapped in pornography and other sexual addiction behaviors. At this point you may be wondering if there is any hope. Let me assure you that the clear, sure, resounding answer is, "YES!"

Steve and I, and all the men we have worked with these many years, are living proof that even the most severe sexual addiction can be healed. We all stand as sure evidence that men in recovery can move forward to experience peace, happiness, fulfillment and most of all—freedom!

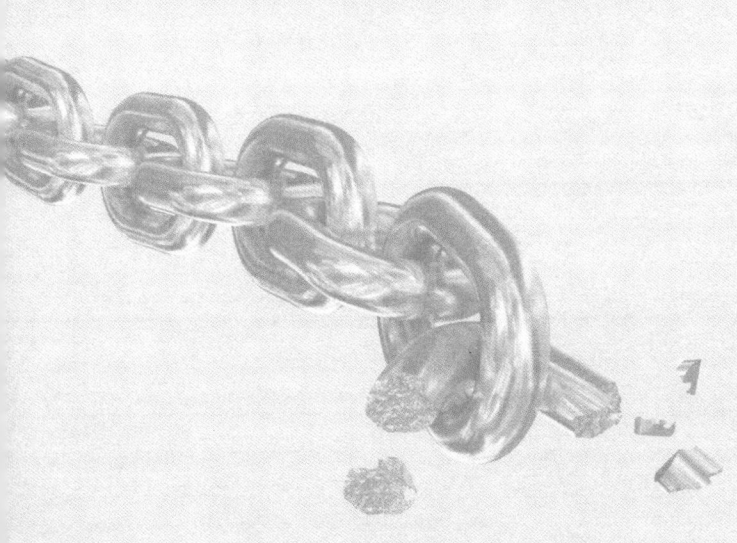

SECTION TWO
THE SOLUTION

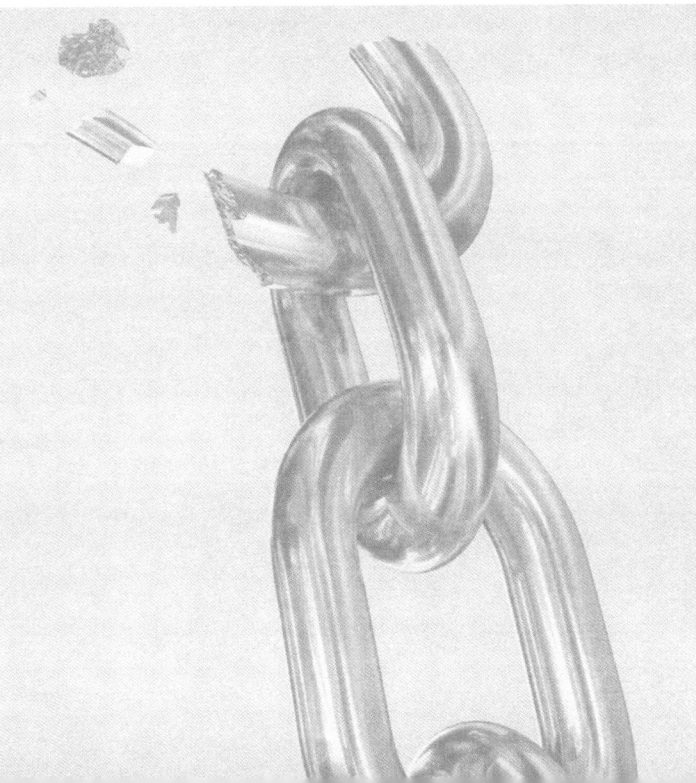

THE ROLE OF ACCEPTANCE AND WILLINGNESS IN LASTING RECOVERY

Stephen Moore

Our brain is a remarkable thing. It has the capability to learn and adapt to ever-changing circumstances. It's able to take perceptions, thought processes and actions, which initially require deliberate action, and develop these into habits. Ever-evolving, the brain is always changing to become more efficient in its work. When I make presentations in front of an audience, for example, many processes are at work simultaneously. I'm walking back and forth while talking. I'm also forming the next thought I will share. Often, I'm operating a projector simultaneous to these tasks. Performing these actions in tandem has become habit; I don't have to think consciously about them.

These marvelous gifts of adapting, habit-forming and change are incredible blessings. Unfortunately, addiction hijacks these God-given abilities. Absent recovery, the thinking patterns, attitudes, ideas and actions that all addicts struggle with become more ingrained over time. The decision processes and thought patterns that proceed our acting out behaviors become automatic. This process makes it difficult for us to recognize how we move progressively from one stage of the addiction to the next, much less prevent ourselves from doing so.

The stakes for a sex addict are high. Lives are at risk. Marriages are teetering on a dangerous ledge. The continued existence of family relationships is on the line. The battle for the soul that pits a man against his addiction is very real and deadly serious. We have outlined the causes, issues and conditions that lead us into sexual addiction and keep us stuck there. Unfortunately, by the time we realize the significance of the problem, we feel beyond rescue. Our repeated attempts to gain lasting sobriety, find inner peace, and quit hiding in shame have taught us that no matter hard we try, we can't break free.

My friends, you must be willing to take the first steps to "unlearn what you have learned." It may seem I am advocating the impossible. Speaking from experience, your situation is not as hopeless as you believe it is. The addiction itself is only half the problem; your *perception* about the situation is the other half.

It Begins with "Radical Acceptance"

The term "radical acceptance" is often used in mental health therapy, and means that we realize truth at the deepest level inside ourselves. When we *radically accept* something, it becomes a reality in both the mind and the heart. For addicts, this process begins with the recognition that our problem is more than a mere obsession; it is an addiction. We cannot escape the evidence all around us: our marriages are failing; we may be facing legal consequences; our acting out only results in more emotional turmoil.

These consequences often push us to change. The more serious they are, the more willing we are to act. As we move toward recovery, we realize more deeply the acuteness of our addiction. We see its impact in our lives and the lives of our loved ones more clearly. The depth of our spiritual disconnection from God becomes readily apparent. With each new step, the scales increasingly fall from our eyes. Mindfulness grows and we begin to see the addiction for what it really is.

Willingness is Vital to Recovery

At this point we also recognize one of the most important truths in recovery: we can't do this alone.

Such was the case for me. I tried everything I could think of to beat this addiction on my own. I preferred death over publicly acknowledging my addiction. I punished myself, taking away privileges after I acted out. Through negative self-talk about how wicked my lust was, I tried to shame myself into change. I tried willpower, or "white-knuckling," to stop this monster on my own. Sadly, we all are pushed to the same inevitable conclusion: if we're going to make lasting change, we need help. We discover that to change, we must *surrender* ourselves to a new way of recovery.

For me and most of my clients, the 12-Step program originally created for Alcoholics Anonymous has been an indispensable part of recovery. One of the most effective components these fellowships have in common is an emphasis on the concept of "surrender." In many cultures, the word "surrender" has a negative connotation, something looked down upon. It is often synonymous in the English language with "giving up," or "giving in." In addiction recovery, the discussion of "surrender" refers to an active choice to proactively let go of something toxic that is limiting progress.

Surrender Is a Necessary Root of the Recovery Tree

While the role of surrender will be discussed in more depth in chapter 11, let's take a look at surrender as a critical step along the path to lasting recovery. Initial surrender in the recovery process is best illustrated with a quote from the literature of Sexaholics Anonymous:

> "I GIVE UP!" It may have come with a loud cry or in a moment of quiet resignation, but the time came when we knew the jig was up. We had been arrested—stopped in our tracks—but we had done it to ourselves. If surrender came only from without, it never 'took.' When we surrendered out of our own enlightened self-interest, it became the magic key that opened the prison door and set us free. Arrest and surrender in order to be set free—what a paradox! But it was

our self-proclaimed freedom that had been killing us, and we began to see that without limits we would destroy ourselves. But we were powerless to limit ourselves, and the more we indulged, the more unmanageable our lives became. Each lustful act or fantasy became another powerful ray penetrating the nucleus of our psyches and loosening the forces that held us together. Thus, in time we came to the growing realization that we were losing control. It was to this truth that we surrendered—the truth about ourselves." (SA White Book, page 83, 2002, "Step One")

At the beginning of recovery, surrender can take many forms, including the decision to work with a therapist, sponsor, or trusted friend to determine which actions are not compatible with recovery. This will involve identifying environments, people, places and emotional states that act as "triggers" to indulge in sexually compulsive behaviors. These include the obvious, such as pornographic websites, strip clubs, and addictive relationships. More subtle triggers may also include feeling depressed, lonely or inadequate. A serious and dedicated recovery journey means developing a greater willingness to either change a relationship with, or eliminate, dynamics and choices that feed the addiction. The best form of surrender is proactive choice, made in both the heart and through action. Surrender is most effective when toxic elements are handed over to someone or something: God, a trusted friend, sponsor or some other form of "higher power."

Surrender begins with the addiction itself, but it doesn't end there. Sobriety is a great beginning, but it is not the ultimate end. The character defects discussed in the first half of this book must be courageously, vulnerably and honestly addressed for lasting, long-term recovery. This process will result in some re-ordered thinking and willingness to continue challenging toxic behaviors and thought patterns. In this way, "surrender" becomes one of many tools available to take back your life.

It's easy to feel overwhelmed and frightened at this point. Addicts, by nature, are reactive, struggle to control their environment, circumstances and people as a way to maintain balance. Changing this approach is not a quick or easy process. Be patient; it will take time to surrender your old reality and begin to adopt a new one. For some, these old ways of thinking are all they have ever known. The process will begin to coalesce in bits and pieces; for now, it's important to begin considering and practicing new ways of thinking and doing things. Seek out those who have found sobriety and recovery, be it peers at a 12-Step group, or a trusted therapist or ecclesiastical leader that you are confident will listen to and support you. As you do, you will begin, as the "White Book" of Sexaholics Anonymous says, "to step into the light, into a whole new way of life." (S.A. White Book, 2001, "The Problem")

RECEIVING GOD'S *UNCONDITIONAL* LOVE AND ACCEPTANCE

Mark Kastleman

WELCOME TO SECTION TWO where the full focus is on "how" to break free from sexual addiction. As we begin, one overarching truth is absolutely vital to your recovery success: You cannot do this without God's help.

Now you may be thinking, "No duh Mark! That's so obvious you really didn't have to mention it." I agree that, on the surface, it appears beyond basic. Yet in my experience, it's apparent that as Latter-day Saints, we complicate, misinterpret and place all kinds of conditions, restrictions and assumptions on this critical keystone principle. This is painfully evident in the questions we sometimes ask ourselves: "Am I worthy of God's help?" "Do I even deserve to be helped?" "Is God so completely disappointed and disgusted with me that He has withdrawn His help so I can suffer for what I've done?" These shame-based questions and doubts, and others like them, illustrate how confused we can become about the nature of God's help.

A more correct and complete word for God's *help* would be God's *grace:* the all-embracing love and all-enabling power that flows to every person through the incomprehensible and infinite Atonement of Jesus Christ. His Atonement was, is and ever will be the most pure and perfect act of love in all the ages of eternity. His Atonement ripples and resonates from the Garden and the Cross to us in this very moment. It empowers, enables, heals, comforts, transforms, covers, reconciles, restores, enlarges, inspires and perfects. It *is* the Grand Key to recovery and permanent freedom from sexual addiction.

Yet, because we view God and ourselves through the twisted *lens of shame*, we refuse to fully receive and utilize the gift of grace. In fact, we often question whether it is an actual gift or something we must partially or fully earn. We will examine that question in great depth in the next chapter. For now, let's explore the *gateway to grace* in the form of a question.

The *Gateway to Grace*

In my recovery program, there is a very pointed question I present to all of my therapy groups. I want to ask you this question, and it's imperative that you be as completely open and honest as possible. Here it is: "Do you believe that your Heavenly Father loves and accepts you without any conditions whatsoever?" Before you read on, please pause and ponder on this question, how it makes you feel and your response.

I have worded the question to take some advantage of the fact that LDS men battling addiction easily drift into thoughts and feelings of deep unworthiness. In my groups I pose the question in exaggerated segments: *Do you believe that your Heavenly Father loves* (long pause) *and* (strong emphasis and pause) *accepts you* (strong emphasis and pause) *without any* (strong emphasis and pause) *conditions whatsoever?*

At the first pause, most begin to shake their heads in the affirmative, reasoning in their minds, "Of course, God loves everyone." But then comes the "and" followed by those unexpected, perplexing words "accepts you." I wish you could gaze through my eyes and see the instant, palpable shift in the faces and body language of my clients when they hear those two words! Certainty turns to doubt; smiles fade or transform into frowns; many heads go down; and an unspoken question permeates the air: "What do you mean, *accepts* me?"

Then of course, things turn completely upside down with the finishing phrase, "without any conditions whatsoever." For most, these words seem almost blasphemous. A lifetime of religious, cultural and doctrinal distortions flood the addict's mind:

> *What do you mean "without any conditions whatsoever"? Of course there are conditions! God expects us to do our part! There are commandments and the exercise of faith and giving service and fasting and praying and reading our scriptures and holding Family Home Evening and keeping the Sabbath day holy and paying tithing and living the Word of Wisdom and magnifying the priesthood and fulfilling our callings and attending the temple and repenting of our sins! And then there's all the despicable, disgusting sexual behaviors I've engaged in over and over again! No conditions? Are you crazy! God only accepts me if I stop sinning and consistently do my best!*

Regardless of how you're feeling in this moment, there is one all-important, deep-as-eternity word that I want you to consider; one that is nearly always misinterpreted or altogether ignored. The word is "you." This is the gateway to grace. How you *see* yourself and how you believe God sees you has everything to do with how successful you will be in accessing and utilizing the power that fuels, sustains and propels your recovery.

The True, Eternal You

During my deep addiction years, looking through the lens of shame and unworthiness, I can tell you exactly how I interpreted the word *you*. If I were asked the question, "Does God love and accept you?" I would have immediately countered with, "You mean does He accept all of my despicable sins, disgraceful choices, foolish mistakes and rebellious behaviors? No way!" I spent decades trying to prove to Him that I was worthy of His love and acceptance. I tried desperately to earn my way back into His grace and, while doing so, separated myself from the very power essential to my recovery and freedom!

Through restored truth and modern revelation, we as Latter-day Saints embrace an eternal perspective, which includes an identity and existence that stretches into the eons before our mortal birth. Yet, when it comes to the question of whether or not God loves and accepts us, the tendency is to immediately measure that query solely against an imaginary tally sheet of successes and failures during this pinprick of time called *mortality*. As you ponder on who you truly are, and how your Heavenly Father and Savior see you, consider this eternal perspective:

> *You are a magnificent Eternal Being who lived with your Heavenly Parents for eons of time in a wondrous place of love, beauty and peace. Under their kind and gentle guidance you learned, progressed and prepared until it was your time and opportunity to come down to this fallen world and enter into a mortal body. And here you are.*
>
> *God intimately knows and loves you in ways that you cannot begin to imagine because you have temporary amnesia. You were just with Him but an instant ago. You have an eternal bond and relationship that was endless ages in the making. He will never abandon, forsake or give up on you—never! And He never stops loving and accepting you, no matter how many mistakes you make.*

I believe that as you increasingly allow yourself to see the true, eternal you, your heart and mind will open to the reality that God does, indeed, love and accept you unconditionally. You are worth every effort required to live free from addiction. You deserve to be happy and at peace. Letting go of resistance and embracing these truths will play a crucial role in your recovery success because you will allow yourself to fully receive and utilize the gift of grace. You'll be willing to do the work of recovery. You will experience increasing desires to think and act like the magnificent son of God that you truly are.

God's Attitude Toward Sin

During a group therapy session, while discussing God's unconditional love and acceptance, a brother in the circle countered with a passionate rebuttal:

> *Hang on just a second, Mark. What about the scripture where God says that He can't look upon sin with the least degree of*

allowance? Are you telling us that God accepts our sinful behaviors and just looks the other way?

This is an excellent example of the challenge we face in separating *who we are* from *the mistakes we've made*. Have you ever pondered on exactly *why* our Heavenly Father cannot look upon sin with the least degree of allowance? What is *sin*? If we go back to the early Hebrew or Greek origins of the word, it means *to miss the mark*. And what is the mark? It is the whole glorious purpose behind why God does everything He does—He loves us perfectly and wants us to enjoy happiness, peace and fulfillment in this world and eternal life in the world to come. In other words, He wants us to have ALL that He has, all that He enjoys, every single part of it! This is the *mark*, and anything that causes us to miss that mark (sin) is in absolute opposition to our Heavenly Father's infinite love and perfect plan. How could He possibly look with any allowance on things that bring us pain, misery and loss?

He does everything He can to help us *hit the mark*. He gives us a map to the mark (commandments and teachings) and a compass to guide us (the Light of Christ and the Holy Spirit). And no matter how many times we stumble and fall; no matter how many errors in navigation; even if we arrogantly, foolishly or rebelliously leave the path, He has provided an infinite and enabling power to cover all of our sins. Christ's Atonement will place us back on track and moving once again toward the mark, if we are willing. The enabling and covering power of Christ's Atonement is accessed through the process of repentance, which literally means to have a *change of mind*. We must *turn* back toward Christ and begin again through His love and grace to follow the straight and sure path to all that our Father has for us.

Of course God cannot accept sin, because it robs us of peace, joy, happiness and fulfillment and causes us to miss the marvelous destination He desires for each of us. But we are magnificent Eternal Beings, loved and accepted by God without condition. He can look upon *us* with every allowance! Don't we constantly stress the gospel principle of *separating the sin from the sinner; hating the sin while still loving the sinner*? Then why, when it comes to how we view ourselves and our own sins, do we have such a difficult time living this directive, and accepting that God lives it?

Some worry that the principle of God loving and accepting us without condition will give permission to addicts to continue acting out: "Hey, God loves and accepts me no matter what so there's no reason to change." The man who uses this rationalization demonstrates that he doesn't know who he truly is. He has allowed his magnificent eternal spirit to be dominated by a fallen robot-ego-brain that has a mind of its own which is complete opposition to God's love and plan of happiness. The man who buys into this attitude shows his extreme emotional and spiritual immaturity, becoming his own enemy and going to war against his own soul and eternal destiny. It means that he is not yet ready to give up his sexual addiction and simply has more to learn, perhaps more to suffer, before he sees the light.

You are NOT Your Addiction!

As you move forward in this section and learn the various tools and principles of recovery, please know that you must begin to change the way you see yourself and the way you believe God sees you. You are a magnificent Eternal Being, a son of God and He loves and accepts you without condition or hesitation! You are NOT your addiction! You are NOT the mistakes of your past! Wasting time and energy in self-flogging, self-hatred and the many forms of shame will only hinder your progress. Embrace God's perfect love and acceptance. Believe that you deserve to be happy and enjoy a life free from addiction—you are worth it! Prepare yourself to fully receive and utilize the precious and priceless gift of grace—*"I can do all things through Christ which strengtheneth me."* (Phil 4:13)

THE GIFT OF GRACE: THE POWER BEHIND YOUR RECOVERY

Mark Kastleman

As you open your heart and mind to God's unconditional love and acceptance, you will naturally begin to feel increasingly open, comfortable and eventually confident in receiving and utilizing the *power* that fuels, sustains and accelerates your daily recovery efforts—*grace*! This power flows directly to you from Jesus Christ through and because of His infinite Atonement. Have you ever wondered *how* Jesus can help you specifically with *your* addiction?

In Doctrine and Covenants section 88 we read: . . . *"He descended below all things, in that He comprehended all things."* And in Alma chapter 7 we find: *"And He shall go forth, suffering pains and afflictions and temptations of every kind . . . and He will take upon Him their infirmities, that His bowels may be filled with mercy, according to the flesh, that He may know according to the flesh how to succor His people according to their infirmities."*

Jesus knows precisely how to help you because He fully comprehends what it feels like to be *you*; to wrestle with *your* unwanted thoughts, urges and behaviors. He knows what it's like to stagger under the heavy burden of *your* sexual addiction because He experienced it personally. In an unfathomable, incomprehensible way, He took upon Himself *your* pains, afflictions, temptations and yes, even *your* addiction, so that He would know exactly how to succor you; exactly how to help you progress on your recovery path and obtain your freedom. This is why He declares in 2 Corinthians chapter 12: "*My grace is sufficient* (completely adequate; enough) *for thee: for my strength is made perfect in [your] weakness.*"

In Matthew chapter 11 He offers what I consider to be the ultimate invitation to you and me; one that resonates deeply in the heart of every addict: "*Come unto me, all ye that labor and are heavy laden, and I will give you rest. Take my yoke upon you, and learn of me; for I am meek and lowly in heart: and ye shall find rest unto your souls. For my yoke is easy and my burden is light.*"

Shackled in the chains of addiction, we are truly *heavy laden*. We *labor* endlessly in our fierce battle with unwanted thoughts, urges and behaviors. How we long for *rest* from the fight and for this crushing burden to become *light*. At times we even dare to dream of a day when we might actually be free. And there in Matthew chapter 11 is the apparent answer: "*Come unto me . . . and I will give you rest.*"

Yet, somehow we just can't figure out *how* to do this! We pray, read our scriptures, attend our meetings, try to obey the commandments, give service and seek to repent of the same addiction behaviors over and over again. Frustration turns to exasperation, then exhaustion and finally hopelessness. We wonder, "Why doesn't grace work for *me*? I know He *can* help me, but why doesn't He?"

First, without someone to show us the way, we really don't know *how* to access Christ's power to overcome addiction in a practical, in-the-trenches, moment-to-moment way. In the chapters that follow, we will learn how to do this. But first, we must be willing to move through the most immediate barrier that stands in our path: the habit of seeing ourselves and our relationship with Christ through a *lens of shame*. We believe that He *can* help us, but question whether He *will* or *why* He doesn't; we believe *in* Him, but have trouble *believing* Him.

I Believe *in* Christ, But I Don't *Believe* Him

My recollection is that it was summertime. I was sitting across the desk from a dear friend and business partner. It was perhaps the deepest and darkest time of my addiction. Dominated by fear and shame, I had gone to great lengths to keep my true struggles a secret. Yet my friend was a deeply spiritual and intuitive soul and suspected that beneath the surface something was seriously amiss. Having just come off an addiction binge, I was wallowing in typical self-flogging, self-condemnation, pessimism, negativity and a full-fledged pity party. After listening patiently to my 20-minute diatribe (with no sharing from me of the actual cause of my distress), he looked me squarely in the eye and firmly declared this stinging rebuke:

> *Do you actually believe you're the only one who has made serious mistakes? Do you honestly think that the guilt and regret and shame you feel are exclusive to you alone? Are you going to sit here and tell me that your sins are so uniquely despicable and special that you have somehow managed to exceed the infinite power of Christ's Atonement; that you have exhausted His infinite love and forced Him to abandon you; that you are the "one" that He cannot and will not save? Shame on you! You are ignorant and arrogant and you need to repent!*

I sat stunned and speechless, completely blind-sided! I remember thinking, "How dare you! I've been pouring out my soul in humble sackcloth and ashes and you treat me like this! Some friend you are!" I silently stood, stoically turned and angrily marched from his office.

For days I steamed and stewed in resentment, anger and denial. But the spirit of God gently and persistently knocked at the heavily barred and barricaded door of my heart. Unwilling to open up more than a tiny crack, the light nonetheless seeped in and gradually I was able to "see." I realized that I had *mistakenly interpreted my pride and shame as humility*. In my blindness, I had placed imaginary limits on the unconditional love and infinite power of the Atonement of Jesus Christ. For the first time in my life I began to admit the truth: that I believed *in* Christ, but I did not *believe* Him.

I could teach *about* grace and the Atonement of Christ from lesson manuals. I could do the research necessary to deliver impressive Sacrament meeting talks on the topic. I could even bear a tearful testimony about my belief in Christ and His sacrifice. But for some reason, I was unable to access His grace from a practical, in the trenches, day-to-day way that over time would free me once and for all from the hell of addiction.

Here is some of the so-called "logic" that often plays on the stage of our minds in relation to God's grace:

1. We believe that we *can* receive God's help, but only *after* we have proven ourselves through a significant amount of our own effort.

2. We want His help, but we also want to keep doing certain things our own way.

3. We believe He *can* help us, but *will* He? Because of our long history of despicable choices, we feel unworthy of His help and therefore doubt He will give it, or how much He will give and for how long.

4. We've prayed and pleaded for His help countless times and yet we're still shackled in addiction. He *can* help us but for some reason He *won't!*

How do we get pulled into this conflict and confusion? I believe it stems primarily from the filter of shame and unworthiness through which we often view God and ourselves. For the balance of this chapter, and the remainder of this book, I invite you to set aside your *shame glasses* and open your eyes to see your Heavenly Father and Beloved Savior in their true nature—through the *lens of grace.* They stand ready and anxious to enable, empower, lift and assist you in every moment, in every step, in every way! And they will provide you with every opportunity to experience, learn, grow and evolve by requiring that you also do *your* part.

Grace: A Gift or Earned? My part vs. His part

One of the great conflicts and confusions I faced during my decades of deep addiction was balancing the *gift* of grace with *my part*. I often wondered, "Is grace a gift from God or do I have to earn it; must I do *my part* first?" I could see this apparent conflict in the scriptures. In Ephesians 2:8 Paul declares, *"For by grace are ye saved through faith; and that not of yourselves: it is the gift of God."* But then in James 2:20, the faithful disciple and half-brother of Jesus boldly announces, *"But wilt thou know, O vain man, that faith without works is dead?"*

From my earliest memories, through my lens of shame and unworthiness, my religious experience seemed to teach that I had to *earn* the gift of grace. Back in chapter 5 of the first section I wrote: *We believed that if we could muster sufficient willpower and sheer grit to remain free from sexually acting out long enough, we could then "earn" our way back into Christ's circle, His love and above all, His acceptance. We had committed to memory the often cited and well-worn scriptural passage, "for we know that it is by grace that we are saved, after <u>all</u> we can do."*

Today, I interpret this verse much differently. Now I understand that even *if* I were able to do <u>all</u> I could do, I would *still* be saved by grace! We cannot *earn* the *gift* of grace. If we have to earn it, then it is no longer a gift. God does not freely offer us grace because we deserve it. In fact it's just the opposite—He gives us His grace because in our weak and fallen state we *need* it; every single child of God is completely lost and doomed without it. However, Christ will not force us to receive and use it, because that would defeat our purpose on this earth: to learn by experience how to use our agency.

During my deep addiction struggles, I often cried out to God, "Why won't you take this from me? Why do you leave me to endlessly struggle and suffer?" Now looking back, I know the answer: God would never rob me of the opportunity to experience, learn and grow by doing *my part* on the road to recovery and freedom. And what is *my part*?

Throughout the chapters that follow, we will share with you the tested and proven tools that we and our clients have used to overcome and live a life free from sexual addiction. Your part is to admit that you cannot do this alone; that doing things "your way" in the past hasn't worked; and to be willing to learn about these tools, actually pick them up and start consistently using them.

However, just as the power tools that line the hardware store shelves are worthless without electricity, *you* must plug into *your* true power source. We can tell you without hesitation or reservation that the underlying, driving power that fuels, inspires, enables and propels you through the recovery process *is* the *gift* of grace through the Atonement of Jesus Christ. This grace not only provides you with the power to work through every aspect of your recovery, it also completely covers you as you make mistakes, stumble, fall and humbly, determinedly rise up to try again and again. This infinite power and mercy is *His part.* This is *how* you and I openly *receive* and *utilize* the *gift* of *grace* as we *yoke* ourselves to Jesus Christ and move forward with Him as a *partner* in our recovery!

ESTABLISHING PHYSICAL, EMOTIONAL AND SPIRITUAL BOUNDARIES WITH YOURSELF

Stephen Moore

As we cultivate the willingness needed for recovery, the changes we must make in our thoughts, interactions with others, and personal conduct become more apparent. As the saying goes: if you continue to do what you've always done, you'll continue to get what you always got. These radical changes take a lot of time and proactive effort; recovery from addiction does not happen passively. For effective recovery, establishing and holding to boundaries becomes the foundation for change.

When we think of the word "boundary," we usually envision a physical barrier; boundaries are meant to keep things out. We build fences to keep the neighbor's dog off our lawn, and lock our doors to keep out intruders who would harm us or our property. These are useful physical structures. But forming good emotional, mental and spiritual boundaries around recovery from sexual addiction requires an understanding that boundaries are just as necessary for *keeping necessary things in* as they are for *keeping harmful things out*.

Clearly Establish End Goals Before Setting Boundaries

While this may seem obvious, it's important to figure out exactly what your goals are in recovery. This includes laying out for yourself what "sexual recovery" is going to look like. Sometimes out of desperation we recognize that we want or need a change in our lives, but don't take the time to spell out the details of what we want that change to look like. While this definition varies from one person to another, I strongly recommend that your basic recovery commitment includes no sexual contact with self or others outside of a healthy marriage relationship.

In my professional work and my own recovery journey, I have yet to see a situation where one can maintain not just sexual sobriety, but lasting recovery from sexual addiction without obeying this basic rule. Real recovery involves cutting out dysfunctional and unhealthy attempts to access sexuality for non-connecting purposes. Using sexuality to escape, numb out, compensate for or cover up emotional stressors or problems will only strengthen your addiction.

By working with a qualified therapist, you will learn how to set more detailed and nuanced boundaries around your sexuality. The goal is eliminating sexual behavior that is disconnecting and feeds your addiction, while finding ways that sex can connect you with your partner and become one part of a fulfilling life.

I Will Do Anything! Well, Almost Anything

Too often, addicts sabotage recovery goals by making "exceptions" to the boundaries that we establish to achieve them. Separating healthy from toxic sexuality takes time, along with trial and error. Setting effective boundaries requires honest self-examination that separates our *needs* from our *wants*. For example, you might be willing to cut out all sexually triggering television shows or movies except a favorite "that just has that one bad part." "I can fast forward or skip that stuff," we often tell ourselves. Can you really? As the saying goes from 12-Step programs: *"Half measures availed us nothing. We stood at the turning point."* (Alcoholics Anonymous Big Book, pg. 59, "How It Works," 2007) My friend, don't fool yourself into thinking that you can insert your own terms into your recovery program and expect real progress. It's likely that attempting to find recovery on your own terms is what got you (myself included) into this mess in the first place. If you're ready to let go of your own way of thinking, then you're ready to set some lasting and meaningful boundaries in your recovery journey.

The "Don'ts" of Recovery

A colleague of mine once compared the impact of addiction, and the collateral damage it creates, to a devastating car crash. Everyone involved walks away emotionally wounded. No one is completely spared. He compared the initial steps of recovery, including setting boundaries with yourself, to "putting yourself in an emotional body cast." It's an apt comparison; a physical cast is meant to restrict movement temporarily so that healing can begin to take hold, with the hope that one day full functioning will return. Establishing the "don't" boundaries restricts our unhealthy thoughts and actions. Like a cast on a broken limb, these boundaries feel restrictive, and they are. We commit to maintaining these boundaries with the long-term hope that real, lasting healing will help us find or reclaim happiness.

Effective boundaries around sobriety are much more complicated than simply saying, "I won't act out sexually again." This is the goal, but addiction means that we can't consistently avoid acting out; our willpower is limited. A commitment to avoid situations, behaviors and attitudes that trigger the desire to act out protects our recovery goals. These boundaries vary from person to person, but some common ones include not accessing the internet without a stated purpose; not watching TV or using the computer while alone; putting a filter on electronic devices, or deleting/cutting off some kinds of social media.

When I discuss these boundaries with my clients, they raise a common concern: "Those are all well and good, Steve, but they won't help me to act differently. I can't go around with a filter on my phone for the rest of my life," or "Never being on the computer alone again isn't realistic."

I respond in two ways. First, these boundaries won't always be or look as restrictive in the long term as they do at the outset of recovery. In many cases, the cast can eventually come off or be swapped out for something less restrictive. Second, telling yourself this isn't realistic in the long-term is simply not true. Many in successful recovery, including myself, *choose* to live with such restrictions even after years of successful recovery. Why, you ask? Because those in long-term recovery have had enough, and they recognize that going back to their old way of life is not an option. It's too miserable, hellish and depressing to do so. Rather than choosing "restrictions," they have elected "freedom" to govern their thoughts and actions and cease being a slave to the impulses of their formerly-addicted selves.

For example, many of the environments that used to trigger me have lost much of their allure. If they can be readily avoided, why would I risk my recovery by tempting fate? Learning to effectively cope with triggering environments, emotions and thought patterns is part of recovery, but it's also important to *pick your battles*. Smart soldiers fight only the essential battles to preserve strength for the times they need it most. Those who go looking for a fight that leaves them weakened or vulnerable are inviting unnecessary danger or even death.

The "Do's" of Recovery

A good recovery plan incorporates many "do's." It isn't enough to simply restrict yourself from activities and situations that are sexually triggering. *This is where we commonly sabotage ourselves in recovery.* If you are going to eliminate particular behaviors or habits as part of recovery, *you must fill that void with productive, positive actions and thought processes.* If you don't, you are inevitably setting yourself up for relapse. Addiction is an emotional security blanket; if we take it away without replacing it with healthy ways of coping, we are doomed to fall back into our old habits.

Common things addicts must "do" include forming a support system that may involve a therapist or sponsor, and connection with others seeking recovery. These support people provide accountability and guidance. Getting regular exercise is another common "do" in recovery; the mental and emotional health benefits are well documented.

It's easy to focus exclusively on the physical boundaries surrounding recovery. But the rules above apply to emotional and spiritual boundaries as well. You will be most successful when you commit to avoid a specific set of triggering behaviors and actions, and seek out new ways to engage in emotionally and spiritually healthy practices. For example, making sure that you are connecting with God on a daily basis is critical. I'm talking about more than prayer and reading scripture. Other helpful practices may include meditation or getting out in nature among God's creations. From an emotional perspective, activities that increase your awareness of what you are feeling and why (we call this mindfulness) are paramount in the recovery process. Daily journaling and meditation, creating gratitude lists and taking time to write about triggers you come across are all emotionally healthy ways of coping with the void left when you shun addictive behaviors.

In the next chapter, we'll discuss how to set and establish boundaries with others. You are on the path to liberation—freedom from addiction! It's a whole new way of living, but you can do it! Mark and I are living proof.

CONNECTING IN HEALTHY WAYS: SETTING BOUNDARIES WITH OTHERS

Stephen Moore

I ONCE HAD A CLIENT (we'll call him Bob) who came to my office having just discovered the significance of his deep-rooted loneliness. Tearfully, Bob relayed to me how terribly alone and abandoned he felt. For most of his life, he had used his sexuality as a substitute for connection with others. Like many of us, the more he turned to his addiction, the more he distanced himself emotionally from others. On the outside, Bob looked like the opposite of loneliness: he had many business contacts, friends and neighbors that he interacted with. However, all of these relationships were very shallow on his end. He was friendly with most people, but was not deeply connected to anyone. He was surrounded by people but felt unseen because he never allowed others to see inside his soul. I worked with him as he slowly came to terms with his emotional isolation, even as he feigned confidence. He was desperate to connect, but terrified to do so. Bob was dying emotionally from the inside out.

Does Bob's story resonate with you? Any commonalities? I have yet to work with an addict that didn't struggle to really connect with others. There is nothing more important in successful recovery than establishing healthy, lasting connection with self, with God, and with others.

On a shelf in my office, I keep a paper mask that I created as part of a psychology class in graduate school. We were tasked with creating a depiction of how we felt inside. I distinctly remember painting each half of the mask a different color, with a line going down the middle; the middle line depicted blood running down the forehead, ridge of the nose, and down the lips and chin; a gory depiction, but an accurate one at the time. You see, though I didn't share it with others then, I was in the very early stages of the recovery process. I was conflicted, with two parts of me raging inside: the broken, wounded, scared, and ashamed inner self which I hated; and the confident, disciplined Christian man, a priesthood leader actively involved at church. The blood running down the middle of the mask represented the way I felt inside. Trying to be both of these people was literally tearing me apart. I was reaching a breaking point. I realized that living behind the mask was no longer going to work. If I was going to get better, I was going to have to open up to others about who I really was and what I really felt. Isolation was killing me, emotionally and spiritually. All of us must learn to take off the mask: with ourselves, with God and with others. This is the only authentic path to connection and freedom. Doing this requires boundaries, not just with yourself, but with those around you.

The Basics: Cutting Out the Incompatible

Before we examine how to connect with others in healthy ways, we must take a deep and ongoing look at our relationships to determine which people, or which internal characteristics, are incompatible with a recovery lifestyle. Lust will be difficult to restrain if we continue to indulge in relationships that feed it. For some of us, this means cutting off relationships with former lovers or affair partners. For nearly all of us, there are other, more subtle culprits that feed our addiction. For example: questionable social media contacts and coworkers who have poor boundaries. In many cases, relationships we need to change or forgo altogether don't involve lust directly. Friends that tell crass jokes, coworkers that encourage or indulge in promiscuity, or those who don't respect our boundaries and our desire to change—all of these threaten successful recovery.

Changing these relationships or cutting them off altogether is an extremely difficult process that takes time. We need the insight of trusted others to recognize which relationships continue to keep us sick and feed our old ways of thinking and acting. In most cases it's not easy to give these up. Part of our addiction is rooted in our emotional dependence on these relationships, dysfunctional though they may be.

I understand this challenge. I had to cut off several relationships in my recovery journey. Even though some of our interactions were positive and uplifting, the emotional cost of continuing these relationships was eroding my recovery process. I was forced to conclude through sad experience that I had to root out unhealthy connections, and replace them with healthy ones. Like Lot and his wife in the Old Testament, it was time to leave my dysfunctional "home" and not look back. Each relationship is different, and making these changes often requires the help of a sponsor and/or therapist. We must ask a vital question: is this relationship bringing me closer to my goal of sobriety and recovery or not? Honesty and mindfulness are both critical in answering this question.

Stick With the Winners

One of many pearls of wisdom that I picked up in early recovery was to practice "sticking with the winners." In other words, you must search out and gravitate to those who have found what you are seeking. One of the best decisions I made was asking my first sponsor if he would be willing to help me. I approached him after sitting next to him for the first time; we'd never spoken before. I had seen him previously at 12-Step meetings and liked what he had to say. He had several years of sobriety, which seemed all but impossible to me at the time. He and I were different in many ways; had I met him in other circumstances, we wouldn't have had much in common. Seeking him out was terrifying. The thought of sharing such a dark and shameful part of myself with a complete stranger was almost unbearable. Yet the prospect of continuing in my addiction was no longer an option. Again and again,

I took the leap that others had invited me to take, and coupled with other actions, began the road to lasting recovery and happiness.

Friends, one of the biggest mistakes many of us make in recovery is attempting the journey alone and without the right people. Many of the people who loved and supported me couldn't provide the direct help I needed. Who can you truly be honest with? Who can you trust to hold your secrets? Your darkest thoughts? Your deepest fears? Who do you know, or are beginning to know, that has walked this road before? These people will be some of your greatest allies in the battle for your freedom, your life and your happiness. For an addict seeking recovery and connection, these associates are worth their weight in gold.

Seize the Day

Radical change is scary. It requires leaving behind the familiar and venturing into the unknown. It's easy to stay in our comfort zone—it's in our nature. Too often, we put off until tomorrow what we should be doing today. How has avoiding necessary change ever helped you? The fact that you are this far into a book on such a personal and uncomfortable topic shows you have the motivation to courageously change. "Tomorrow" will never come until you make it "today." Take that first step. Don't worry about the journey—just move one foot forward. Now. *Today.* You can do it!

YOU ARE **NOT** YOUR BRAIN!

Mark Kastleman

Earlier in the book I quoted a friend who expressed the immense frustration we feel in battling addiction:

When my addiction urge would hit, it was like another totally separate person would take over. That guy didn't care about anyone or anything except his sexual goal. He was completely narrowed and calculating and unfeeling. When the acting out was done, it was like my real self would wake up and come back into focus.

Every addict knows the bewildering phenomenon of feeling like "there's two of me inside one body!" In fact, that sensation is based on the truth that we are all *dual beings:* a glorious, intelligent *eternal spirit* dwelling temporarily inside a magnificent but fallen *mortal body*. And within that body is a remarkable, centralized supercomputer known as the *human brain*.

The brain is a marvel and a wonder. It weighs a little over three pounds, making up just 2 percent of the body's weight, but uses 20 percent of the body's blood and oxygen. This little supercomputer houses all of the thoughts, experiences, learning, feelings, emotions, interactions and interpretations you have ever experienced; a vast info database indeed! Yet, as magnificent as your brain is, it is a closed, *finite* system of information and memories. "It" only knows what "it" knows, nothing more.

But *you* are an *Eternal Being*. You have always existed, just as Jeremiah of old to whom the Lord declared, "*Before I formed thee in the belly I knew thee; and before thou camest forth out of the womb I sanctified thee, and I ordained thee.*" (Jer 1:5) When you die and your brain lies six-feet-under with worms crawling through it, *you* will continue to exist, think, reason, feel and remember. Therefore, *you are NOT your brain!*

The Eternal You vs. the Fallen Brain

Many people scurrying about each day have no idea they are *dual beings*. Few pause to discern and distinguish the conjured thoughts of their fallen brains from the light and truth of their eternal spirits. Most take for granted that the thoughts or emotions they experience in the moment *are* reality. They believe that they *are* their thoughts and feelings and allow these to dictate how they react, respond, behave and choose to live their lives. A key to your recovery success lies in your openness and willingness to begin *seeing* your conjuring brain for what *it* is, and distinguish *it* from the true *Eternal You*.

The battle to attain a level of awareness where you can discern between your fallen brain and your true self is nothing new. Your ancient brothers in the priesthood wrestled just as you do. In Romans 7, Paul laments: "*O wretched man that I am! Who shall deliver me from the body of this death?*" And earlier in the same chapter he declares: "*For the good that I would I do not: but the evil which I would not, that I do.*" In the Book of Mormon, Nephi mourns a similar struggle: "*O wretched man that I am! Yea, my heart sorroweth because of my flesh; my soul grieveth because of mine iniquities.*" (2 Nephi 4:17)

During the October 1993 General Conference, Elder F. Enzio Busche delivered a remarkable talk titled, "Truth is the Issue." I failed back then to see the pure genius of it, but I fully appreciate it today:

> As our mind is opened through our study of the plan of salvation, each of us comes to see that our life means that the "real me," or "the spiritual child of God," created in innocence and beauty, is engaged

in a fight for life or death with the elements of the earth, the "flesh," which, in its present unredeemed state, is enticed and influenced by the enemy of God. Our brain, the great computer where all the facts of life's memories are held together, can also be programmed by the "flesh," with its self-centered ideas to deceive the spiritual self.

The issue is truth, my dear brothers and sisters, and the only way to find truth is through uncompromising self-education toward self-honesty; to see the original "real me," the child of God, in its innocence and potential. [This is]in contrast to the influence from the other part of me, "the flesh," with its selfish desires and foolishness.

Left to itself, your brain will always pursue its default biological programming: to survive at all costs. The brain is selfish and self-centered by its very design. This is why when faced with people, situations, circumstances or feelings that it interprets as threatening, painful, shameful, awkward, uncomfortable or stressful, it will seek escape, avoidance and self-soothing. With time, experience and repetition, a certain outlet can become your brain's favorite "go-to-place" and easily evolve into an addiction. This is why we refer to the brain as having an "ego" because "it" seeks to do things "its" way, thus *edging God out (ego)*. Effective recovery requires that you learn how to stand back as an observer and *watch* your brain without being deceived and lured in.

Become a Watcher: *Act* Instead of Being *Acted Upon*

One of the most extreme examples of the computer-ego-brain completely overruling and dominating the eternal spirit is in the lives of Laman and Lemuel in the Book of Mormon. You have to wonder if these two brothers had any idea they were Eternal Beings temporarily dwelling within a fallen body. Their father, Lehi, labored in vain to help them see their eternal nature. In 2 Nephi 2: 14 and 16, he revealed powerful truth: *"And now, my sons, I speak unto you these things for your profit and learning; for there is a God, and he hath created all things, both the heavens and the earth, and all things that in them are, both things to act and things to be acted upon. Wherefore, the Lord God gave unto man that he should act for himself."*

Unlike Laman and Lemuel, you can become a *watcher* of your thoughts and urges. You can stand back and observe, direct and manage the stage of your conscious mind. You can "act" as opposed to being constantly "acted upon." In the chapters that follow, you will learn how to recognize your ego-brain's arsenal of tactics intended to keep you trapped in addiction. You will learn how to use a host of tools and develop the necessary skills to rule over your brain as opposed to allowing it to rule over you. Here's a simple tool to get you started:

The Forceful Stage Director

Think of your conscious mind as a *stage*. Your thoughts are the *actors* on that stage and *you* (your true Eternal Self) are the stage *director*. You are in charge! You get to decide which actors (thoughts) are allowed to stay and play on your stage and which ones must leave.

Here's how to use this tool: whenever you notice an unwanted thought or urge trying to force its way onto the stage of your mind, immediately put your hand up and firmly issue the command "STOP!" If you're alone, say it out loud. If other people are near, say it forcefully in your mind. Then, with a very stern, dominant voice declare, "This is the stage of MY mind and there is NO place for that here!"

Next, ask yourself a very simple question, "If there is no place for that thought on my stage, then what kind of thought is there a place for?" Often, a replacement thought or idea will come to you: immediately allow it in and shift all of your attention there. If something doesn't come, simply ask, "Heavenly Father, where do I need to place my thoughts right now?" Pause and quietly wait for an impression to come and then shift.

Once you shift your thoughts, don't just sit or stand there! Get moving by engaging in another recovery tool or simply get back to the task at hand. The stage director tool is designed for a quick shift of thought. You must follow it up with other activities so that you don't become trapped in an *avoidance cycle*. (See Section One, chapter 12).

You are NOT your Brain!

Remember, no matter what kind of unwanted thoughts or urges you're facing, no matter which recovery tools you're implementing, always seek the place of *awareness*—an awareness of *who you truly are!* You are NOT your computer-ego-brain. You are a magnificent, intelligent Eternal Being, enabled and empowered by the grace of Jesus Christ. YOU can always stand back, observe and watch "it" (your brain) and then subject "it" to what is good and right and true. You can *act* as opposed to being *acted upon*.

CLEARING AWAY THE WRECKAGE OF YOUR PAST

Stephen Moore

MALAD, IDAHO, is a typical small American town, one of many similar towns that dot a rural western landscape. It's a place I have thought about often but, until recently, had never visited. Malad is a place where the course of my life was altered; home to one of the greatest losses a 12-year-old boy could experience. In 1996, a private plane carrying eight good men, one of them my father, crashed into a hillside just outside Malad, killing everyone aboard.

Each time I drove by Malad on I-15, I always had a "surface" reason for not visiting the crash site: not enough time, it's too far away, not even knowing if anything is still there. The real reasons, though, ran much deeper. For a long time, it was because of my anger and rage at the injustice of what had happened there. For years after the crash, it was because of the sadness and loss. I'm grateful to say that in recent years I was able to drive by without recalling the trauma of the place.

Yet I realized in 2017 that it was important to make the trip. Doing what I could to face this place and the emotions I had tied up with it represented the next step in finding acceptance and peace around such a difficult part of my life. You see, as devastating as the loss of my father was, the long-term implications of what happened there stretch much further and much deeper than the loss itself (a story for another time). For me, Malad had always represented the physical "ground zero" of my nearly twenty-year journey into the web of addiction, and all of its subsequent consequences. What happened just outside Malad is the genesis of my addiction past.

I finally visited the crash site in summer 2017 with my mother and my wife. Had I not known specifically where I was going, I wouldn't have recognized the place when we arrived. No signs of the accident were visible from the dirt road that led up into the foothills. My preparation included a lot of research and digging for details about the accident. With the passage of time, I had to actually excavate the soil to find remnants of the plane. And so it is in our lives when it comes to emotional trauma. Events long in the past can create a distortion of memory. After years of trying to forget, the trauma is often difficult to identify. On the surface, it may even appear as if there is no wound there. Like the remnants of plane wreckage at the crash site, the emotional wreckage that lies at the heart of our addiction is lurking just under the surface.

You Can't Change What You Can't See

Before you can begin to remove the roots of your addiction, you have to be able to uncover and identify them first. This process is a journey, and one that is not effectively taken alone. On that Idaho hillside, I found some debris on my own, but much of what I discovered would have remained hidden without my support system—the people I had with me. I would have simply overlooked much of it. This is a critical reason for developing a support system on the road to recovery: we need others to help us to see what we can't see alone. We all have emotional "blind spots" that we can't identify ourselves.

I can speak to this personally. I am a therapist; I specialize in working with trauma, addiction and betrayal. I have significant training and experience. Many consider me to be an "expert" in these fields. *Yet I still see a therapist on a regular basis.* We all need the help of loving, understanding and knowledgeable people who can guide us in our journey. Most of us have spent too much time trying to tackle the difficult tasks of recovery on our own. Now is the time to change that.

Clearing Away the Wreckage of Your Past

Inside the circle of 12-Step programs, you will often hear about the need to "clear away the wreckage of your past" in order to find long-term healing and recovery. (Alcoholics Anonymous, "Big Book", pg. 164) How true this is! As I looked closer and began digging through that patch of Idaho hillside and scanning it with a metal detector, it didn't take long to find relics from my painful past: a twisted piece of metal here, a jagged bent portion of a seat there. I also noticed that, as I looked closer, much of the evidence of the crash on the surface was still present. Not as many shrubs and plants grew there, likely a result of the jet fuel, chemicals and other debris that remained in the soil. *The wreckage from a crash two decades earlier was continuing to affect the landscape.*

Many years ago, I worked with a couple that had been married more than 20 years. He (we'll call him James) had a past history of acting out in sexual addiction, though he had been free of doing so for well over a decade. She (we'll call her Amy) had discovered his addiction by accident 15 years before they visited my office, and had been devastated at that time. They had seen a therapist briefly upon her discovery. Among other things, that therapist counseled them to establish a regular schedule for physical intimacy as a part of their marriage therapy.

Fast-forward ten years; James and Amy came to see me for the first time. The week prior, Amy had experienced a significant emotional trigger resulting from James' behavior (something unrelated to his addictive past), one which took her back to the time when he was in active addiction. She immediately shut down, both emotionally and physically. Despite James' efforts to make amends, she was insistent that James move out, and that divorce was imminent.

I began working with them, both individually and as a couple. I spent some time at the beginning doing "damage control" sessions, helping them establish basic boundaries, a self-care routine, and rules for effective communication. Then we began to look at why Amy had reacted so acutely, despite her husband's decade of sobriety. As I worked with Amy, we discovered a couple of things. First, Amy had never really dealt with her husband's betrayal 15 years prior. Having ended therapy prematurely, she buried most of the anger, hurt, guilt, shame and insecurity that stemmed from those devastating events.

Second, both James and Amy had grown up in very emotionally neglectful and abusive households. Neither had ever learned how to really love or connect with another person because it had not been modeled for them. Both were emotionally fragile, and their marriage had been somewhat rocky from the beginning. This was even more evident following James' sexual betrayal. On the surface, things had looked positive. Most observers would have seen the typical couple, with the typical family and friends. Together, we began the journey of healing; both of them had a long way to go. After much therapy and hard work, they made significant progress, and are now in the process of building the marriage they have always wanted.

Beginning the Journey

The process toward healing often begins because of pain: things have become so difficult that change is the only option. You must change or you will lose everything. The next step is seeking help to begin the process of understanding how to stop acting out sexually (covered in other chapters). Just as important is the quest to understand *why* an addict feels the need to act out in the first place. Is sex pleasurable? Of course. But our addiction-related problems go so much deeper than a simple overdrive for sexual activity. *A person does not engage in sexually compulsive and destructive behavior despite the risk to his family, church membership, career and himself unless he is running, covering up, or coping with some significant, underlying problem.*

Once you find sobriety and have started the process of identifying what makes your addiction tick, you work with those around you to slowly dig up and examine the "wreckage." *The journey of confronting your past is also a large part of the process of accepting yourself in the present.* Be courageous in seeking help. Be patient with yourself as you do so. If you are like virtually every man I have worked with, you are not crazy. You are not a deviant. *You are in pain.* Your growth and progress is being hindered, not simply because you struggle to say "no" to your drug, but because *you are running from your addiction's true origins*. Recovery starts the first time you show up to a support group; the first time you pick up the phone and reach out to another who is struggling like you are; or make a phone call to a therapist. What will be your first step to your Idaho hillside? Perhaps it's reading this book. Keep reading, my friend. You're on the right track.

WALKING THROUGH WALLS: HEALING THE CORE CAUSES OF ADDICTION

Mark Kastleman

SEXUAL ADDICTION is a quick fix the brain uses to escape, cover over and soothe deep, uncomfortable, difficult and painful core issues. In essence, addiction is only a *symptom* of the actual underlying *dis-ease*. If we only treat the surface while ignoring the core cause, addiction will continue rearing its ugly head over and over again. I want to share an allegory that has helped me and many of my clients understand this essential part of recovery. It was inspired by one of my favorite spiritual teachers, Guy Finley (guyfinley.com) and I call it *Walking Through Walls*.

Walking Through Walls

Imagine for a moment a man (we'll call him John) who has a desperate, burning desire to overcome his sexual addiction. John has started to realize that his addiction is only a symptom of deeper issues, but he's not sure how to proceed. One day in deep meditation, he finds himself walking peacefully on a beautiful mountain meadow trail. Suddenly, the earth begins trembling violently, knocking him to his knees. Directly before him, thrusting its way up and out of the ground, a massive cement wall emerges, blocking his path. It looms so high and wide there are no visible boundaries. He cannot go over, under or around it. In frustration, he pounds his fist on the dull gray surface only to encounter solid rock. He wields his pocketknife and scrapes at the wall with little effect. Unable to advance, he dejectedly executes an about face and starts off in the opposite direction.

A few minutes later, the event replicates itself, leaving him once again face to face, not simply with another insurmountable wall, but the *same* knife-scraped monolith! Utterly exasperated, he stomps off only to encounter the identical experience again.

Throughout the day, an endless *déjà vu* unfolds until eventually he sinks exhausted down into the dirt, his back propped hopelessly against the relentless wall. Then suddenly the earth trembles again, yet his wall remains motionless. To his astonishment, about 50 yards ahead and to his left he sees a man standing in front of a massive wall similar to his own! Recovering from his initial amazement, he muses to himself, "I wonder how he'll handle the same challenge I've been facing all day?"

He watches anxiously as the man squarely faces the wall and gently runs his hands over it, seeming to explore every crack and crevice. Then, he calmly turns and walks away. John exults, "I knew it! I knew he would eventually turn and walk away just like me!" But a few minutes later, the man returns carrying a bucket with a huge wire brush and several rags. Completely perplexed, John wonders, "What in the world is this guy up to?" The man calmly, deliberately picks up the wire brush and begins vigorously scraping on the cement wall. Certain the man is insane, John nonetheless continues his observation.

At first John doesn't believe his eyes, but gradually, undeniably, the scraping begins to have an obvious effect: a deepening indentation appears, taking the shape of a crude arched doorway. Working steadily, tirelessly, the man labors on, hollowing out a sizeable alcove. Before breaking entirely through the wall, the man discards the wire brush and, taking up the rags, begins wiping and buffing the remaining cement surface. "What can he possibly be attempting now?" John mutters. Then John begins to see it, faint at first, but gradually growing until in shimmering brilliance stands a mirror!

Dropping the rags, the man retreats several steps and stands motionless with his arms outstretched gazing peacefully, acceptingly at his own reflection in the looking glass. After what seems like days, the man smiles and begins moving slowly, confidently toward the mirror. John tenses at the moment he is certain the man will collide face first with the shiny barrier, but to his complete astonishment, in one fluid motion, the man passes effortlessly, elegantly through! And in the same instant, the great gray wall itself vanishes from sight, leaving only the sound of the man's soft footsteps fading into the distance!

What are *Your* Walls?

During my decades of addiction struggle, I was so completely besieged by the daily inner warfare, the in-your-face symptoms that I was unable or unwilling to step back, open my eyes and *see* the underlying core issues; the *walls* obstructing my forward progress, recovery and freedom.

I recall a moment of breakthrough when my wise and loving mentor, Dr. Page Bailey, firmly stated, "Mark, sexual addiction is NOT about sex, any more than alcoholism is about the liquid in the glass." At first I bristled in resistance to this seemingly obvious contradiction. But then Page began helping me explore these all-important questions: "Why do I seek to avoid, escape and self-medicate through pornography and other sexual outlets in the first place? Is it just about naked bodies and climax, or is there something more profound happening?"

As I began to dig down to the deeper issues, the view wasn't pleasant or easy; it often stabbed at my ego-brain. Over the years, many different walls (issues) were revealed to me. Here are just a few:

- *Seeking to soothe the pain of childhood traumas and abuse.*
- *Acting self-righteous, perfectionistic, or "always right" to hide feelings of inadequacy, unworthiness and shame.*
- *Seeking pleasure over accepting responsibility and doing hard things.*

- *Emotional immaturity—avoiding and escaping rather than confronting people and situations head-on.*
- *A tendency toward being negative and pessimistic.*
- *Easily defaulting to doubt, fear and an obsession with "what-ifs."*
- *Judging, criticizing and finding fault in others.*
- *Putting on masks (often professional or religious) to keep people from seeing the "real me" with all of my weaknesses and flaws.*
- *Various levels, often subtle, of dishonesty, duplicity and "white lies."*
- *Behaving in selfish and self-centered ways.*
- *Feeling jealousy and envy toward others I perceived to be more successful, righteous or blessed than me.*
- *Keeping secrets and going to elaborate lengths to conceal my addiction behaviors from family and friends.*

As I began *seeing* these walls, at first I tried the quick solution of going over, around, under or simply busting my way through them. When these attempts failed, I would often give up and retreat back to the temporary refuge of my addiction. But predictably, inevitably, the same walls kept rising up to barricade my way again and again.

Working to Transform Your Walls Into Mirrors and then Doorways

Like John in our allegory, you must be willing to take up your *wire brush* and vigorously engage in the daily labor of scraping on your wall to reveal what your survival-dominated, pain-avoiding ego-brain has worked so hard to cover over and hide deep within. Over time, you will begin to see your own reflection in that wall: the raw, real and vulnerable *you* with all of your weakness and pain.

As you continue the work of recovery, you will use your *buffing rags* to gradually improve the clarity of your view, until standing before your *mirror*, you will see the full truth of the thing that has been holding you back. Without shame, denial or avoidance, enabled and empowered by the grace of Christ, you will use your recovery tools. Over time you'll find healing and resolution, until finally you are ready to simply *walk through your wall* and move on. In the chapters that follow, Steve and I will share some of the tools that we and our clients have used to succeed in this process.

One question I am often asked is, "What happens when I've worked through all of my walls?" You will recall at the end of the allegory, the man's wall disappeared and he walked peacefully off into the distance. However, if you were to follow him on his path of recovery and life, you would find him facing yet another wall—not the same wall, but a new one. Until some future day in the eternities when you have finally evolved into your wholeness, completeness and *perfection*, there will always be new walls rising up in your path. These walls are your teachers. They reveal to you all that you must *move through* to continually grow and progress. With practice and experience, you will come to appreciate these walls and see them not as a curse, but as a gift. I love the Lord's promise in Ether 12:27 regarding the walls (gifts) that He gives us:

"And if men come unto me I will show unto them their weakness [walls]. I give unto men weakness [walls] that they may be humble; and my grace is sufficient for all men that humble themselves before me; for if they humble themselves before me, and have faith in me, then will I make weak things become strong unto them [they will walk through walls]."

EGO-BRAIN TENDENCIES VS. ETERNAL SELF ATTRIBUTES

Mark Kastleman

UNCHECKED AND LEFT TO ITSELF, the fallen human brain always defaults to its natural programming of selfishness, self-preservation, self-protection, self-serving, self-centeredness, pleasure-seeking, pain-avoidance, etc. The brain with its built-in EGO (edge God out) always seeks to do things "its" way, according to "its" will.

One of the most challenging aspects of recovery for you and me is voluntarily evolving to a place of brutal self-honesty where we can directly confront and openly admit the fact that we have allowed our ego-brains to take over our lives and keep us trapped in addiction. We have given over the management of our problems, challenges, stresses, doubts and fears to the computer between our ears that has a *mind of its own*—a closed system that only *knows what it knows* and tends to shut itself off from the *mind of God*. We allow "it" to transform us as Eternal Beings into avoiders, escape artists and pleasure-seekers. This is why God describes the *natural man* (ego-brain) as His *enemy*. In other words, the ego-brain is at *enmity* with Him: actively opposed, separated from, hostile toward.

When allowed to dominate and *take the wheel*, the ego-brain has a certain way of reacting to the people, circumstances and events going on around it; a vast arsenal of strategies and tactics I call *Ego-Brain Tendencies* or *EBTs*. They have also been described as *character defects* or *character liabilities*. Because the brain's very nature and programming is completely selfish and self-absorbed, many of these EBTs are negative and destructive. The brain easily employs these tendencies rather than take on what it perceives as the more difficult, uncertain and intimidating task of facing people and life in healthy, mature, inspired ways. Of course, when we allow the ego-brain to immerse itself in these tendencies, the natural consequences follow and our lives become unmanageable and downright difficult. At this point the brain seeks to escape through its favorite sexual outlets; it seeks to escape and self-medicate the very consequences it created in the first place!

Ego-Brain Tendencies (EBTs)

Be aware that your ego-brain will do everything it can to hide its EBTs from you. You must be willing to stand and boldly, humbly face these *walls* and begin scraping away until you can clearly and completely *see* the full reflection of these tendencies staring back at you. You must be willing to take full *response–ability* for them; to do the consistent, daily work required to move *through* them; and replace them with healthy, mature, inspired behaviors.

You may be wondering, what exactly are these EBTs? They are vast and varied, but here's a good list to start with:

Self-Pity	Laziness	Catastrophizing
Self-Justification	Procrastination	Denial
Self-Condemnation	Insincerity	Minimizing
Dishonesty	Negative Thinking	Intellectualizing
Impatience	Immoral Thinking	Avoidance
Anger	Criticizing	Diversion
Resentment	Shame	Apathy
Pride	Fear	Spiritualization/Religiosity
Jealousy	Judgmental	Terminal Uniqueness
Envy	All or Nothing Thinking	Blaming Others

Eternal Self Attributes (ESAs)

The good news in all of this is: YOU are NOT your brain! You are a magnificent Eternal Being created in the image of God. You possess *Divine DNA*—all of the attributes of God in embryo. In your Eternal Home before this life, over eons of time, you developed many *Eternal Self Attributes* or *ESAs* to various levels and degrees, and brought them with you! As an essential part of God's perfect plan, you cannot remember *who* you truly are: your true Eternal Self. That's why He gave you the light of Christ, the Holy Spirit and His written word—to remind you of your ESAs. Consider this beginning list:

Love	Forgiveness	Seeking to Understand
Submissiveness	Trust	Measured Reactions
Meekness	Appreciation	Trusting in God
Humility	Gratitude	Accepting Responsibility
Letting Go	Peacefulness	Telling the Whole Truth
Letting God	Gentleness	Feeling with your Heart
Proactive Accountability	Joyfulness	Facing it Head On
Self-Acceptance	Sincerity	Transparency
Honesty	Optimism	Connection/True Intimacy
Patience	Empathy	Gentleness
Kindness	Faith	
Compassion		

Your Daily Personal Inventory

A key to recovery is to become increasingly aware of your EBTs and develop the skill of shifting and replacing them with ESAs—your truest way of thinking and behaving. A direct and practical tool to achieve this is through the *Daily Personal Inventory*. Here are some simple steps to implement this powerful tool:

1. Prior to retiring for the night, take some quiet, focused time to reflect back on your day.

2. In prayer, humbly ask God to help you recognize the various EBTs that were at work in your thoughts, intentions and interactions over the last 24 hours.

3. Review the list of EBTs and give each one a score according to how prominent a role you feel it played: 3 = Major; 2 = Medium; 1 = Minor; 0 = not at all, or you were able to shift from the EBT to an ESA in the moment.
4. After giving yourself a score for each EBT, choose one of your highest scoring EBTs to focus on over the coming 24 hours.
5. Choose one ESA that you will use to replace the selected EBT.
6. Record the EBT and ESA on your smartphone or on a 3x5 card and carry it with you.
7. Strive to be aware of any time the EBT enters the stage of your mind. When it does, firmly issue the command, "STOP!" and immediately bring the idea and feeling of the ESA into your mind, consciously *shifting* to the thoughts and behaviors that match that ESA.
8. Keep track of your EBT scores over time to spot trends, areas for focus, and celebrate your progress. You can also score your daily ESA list to help you notice and acknowledge your forward progress.

Be Prepared for Ego-Brain Resistance!

As you begin boldly, humbly and honestly looking at your EBTs and replacing them with ESAs, be prepared for the ego-brain to resist and rebel. It doesn't like the spotlight shining on all of its weaknesses and flaws. And it especially detests the idea that you might actually address the underlying core issues so that there is no longer a need to keep turning to sexual outlets for escape and self-medication. Be prepared for the ego-brain *chatter* or *self-talk* that will sound something like this:

- *This addiction isn't about what's going on inside of me! It's all the negative people and circumstances around me that are creating my problems and my need to escape.*

- *I can overcome this addiction without doing all this touchy-feely inner work.*

- *Yep, once again the focus is on everything that's wrong with evil, pathetic, loser me!*
- *Why bother? I know I'll never overcome this. I always fall back into it. What's the point?*
- *Fine, I'll give it a try but I know it won't work. I'll do it to get people off my back.*
- *What exactly am I supposed to do when life just gets overwhelming or my wife isn't responsive—I can't make it without my release valve.*

While it's true that initially your brain will seek to *protect its turf* and resist your efforts to uncover the core issues that drive your addiction, God has already built into your brain a wonderful system and structure for change. It's called *neuroplasticity*, which means your brain is moldable and shapeable; it's *plastic*.

Through consistent repetition over time, this neuroplasticity has allowed your brain to build up a whole list of EBTs and the wiring and circuitry for addiction. Using the same principle, you can direct the process of building up your ESAs and shrink your addiction wiring. In essence, the same type of brain processes that got you into your addiction can help get you out. In Romans 12:2, Paul beautifully describes God's gift of neuroplasticity: *"And be not conformed to this world: but be ye transformed by the renewing of your mind, that ye may prove what is that good, and acceptable, and perfect, will of God."*

As you begin peeling back the layers of shame and secrecy to reveal and heal the core causes of your addiction, be patient and hold on to hope. The process will neither be easy nor brief, but with daily repetition over time, enabled and empowered by grace, you will be *"transformed by the renewing of your mind."*

HOLDING YOURSELF ACCOUNTABLE WHILE ACCEPTING YOUR HUMANITY

Stephen Moore

We have identified negative traits and characteristics that are nearly universal in sexual addiction. Like Hansel and Gretel, these traits often come in pairs (or even large groups), holding hands as they skip down the primrose path to danger. They contribute to and feed off each other. Among the most common of these traits is the inability to trust anyone or anything. *Trust* plays an integral role in both addiction and recovery. Many of us have been let down or hurt by people and events from our past, and each of us is guilty of hurting ourselves in our addiction. We don't trust that anyone will accept us for who we really are. We struggle to trust our Creator—that He can and will catch us when we fall. Perhaps most of all, we struggle to trust ourselves. We've let ourselves and others down so many times that we've lost count. Some have lost all hope of recovery.

As addicts, our ability to trust ourselves is impaired. We struggle to consistently say no to our addiction. We can't trust ourselves not to hurt those we care about, nor can we rely on ourselves to succeed in a variety of circumstances. If you're reading this book, it's likely that you are so mired in shame, guilt, and thinking errors that your ability to see yourself as you really are is all but non-existent. And that's okay! Recovery doesn't begin with trusting yourself; that will come in time. It begins with trusting others.

Healthy Accountability Starts With Others

Accepting this reality about trust is difficult but necessary. If you recognize that you need to change, you must begin to shift your thinking. In the past, trusting your own judgment hasn't taken you very far on the path to recovery. *Addicts are overly critical of themselves on one extreme, and justify horrible actions and activities on the other.* It's time for a radical shift in thinking. You must begin to trust those close to you when it comes to evaluating yourself and your progress in recovery. Others who understand your struggle and are able to see what needs to change, as well as see the good in you, are critical to your success. These often include trusted family members or friends, but in particular, they should include others on the same journey toward successful recovery.

A Constant and Deliberate Choice

I work with many men who get better and break free from their addiction. They make progress at varying speeds and along different paths. One client whom we will call Jesse, a man in his 60s, made some of the most rapid progress I have ever witnessed. When I first met him, his marriage was on the brink of the abyss. He hated himself to the point of engaging in self-harm, and had lost much of his will to live. Compared to others in his therapy group, his addiction was the most acute. Yet over the course of nine months, I saw him make more rapid progress, find more sobriety, and obtain the most significant change of anyone in the group. Why? He was willing to trust deeply—to abandon his own thinking and completely turn over not just his actions, *but his heart and limited willpower* to those willing to help him.

Every week he would ask questions. Every time we met he would take notes. Every time he was discouraged, he chose to trust me when I offered encouragement and told him he was doing well. If I had told Jesse to dig trenches in order to stay sober, I am certain he would have done it. He had not just a willingness to change; *he made a daily, active choice to trust what those around him were telling him, while at the same time choosing to ignore his destructive inner voice.* You know what I mean when I say "inner voice," don't you? It's the voice that tells you how worthless you are; that you will never change; that no one will ever love and accept you. It's the same voice that justifies your choice to act out, only to shame you mercilessly the minute you do. It's the voice of emotional insanity and mental delusion. It's the voice of your addiction, coupled with those unseen forces that want you to fail.

Recovery begins with learning to ignore that voice! It is a conscious, deliberate action that you must practice day to day, even hour to hour in the beginning. Every time you hear that voice, you must immediately refocus your thoughts with help from someone you trust. Someone who loves you. Someone who cares. Someone who will help you see where you can improve and accurately share with you the progress they observe—the things you are doing well. This is a role you can't play for yourself, and the reason connection is so critical in the recovery process.

Accountability Relearned

I don't know about you, but I'm an expert at honestly critiquing myself; finding my flaws; identifying areas where I'm doing poorly. At least I thought I was. Contrary to what you may have learned in church culture or through other societal cues, honest accountability isn't simply examining areas where we need to improve. Society tends to measure progress by focusing on what is lacking, and we do the same with ourselves. Add the deep shame addicts all carry into the mix, and it's easy to see how we focus exclusively on our flaws and mistakes.

Productive accountability involves an honest, accurate assessment of both weaknesses *and* areas of improvement. It includes an accurate view of your strengths and assets, as well as an understanding of your eternal identity and the practice of self-compassion.

When clients come to my office for the first time, they often see themselves as less valuable than the chair they sit in. After listening for years to that critical inner voice, they have lost the ability to see their addiction clearly, and they can't see any hint of their eternal worth and potential. They have been duped into thinking that they can't change because *they are not worthy* to do so. Past trauma wounds reinforce this way of thinking.

My view of clients is much different. I see them as kings, heirs and eternal beings with a divine inheritance. Each is a treasure both to God and to the people who love him. Recovery is not just about changing into something new; it's also about *rediscovering what you have been all along*. You see yourself as flawed, broken, weak, and a weight on those around you, but I see a priceless gem whose infinite worth has always been there, but is hidden beneath the tarnish of shame, addiction, trauma and self-loathing. You must trust others to help polish you so you can see yourself not simply as an addict, but as a person of infinite value. Learn to accept your humanity and realize that these trials, overwhelming as they seem, are stepping stones in a much bigger, much grander journey. You must learn to trust again. Step by step, small gains help such trust to grow, and the tiniest seedling of trust can grow into the strongest of tree of confidence.

STOP DOING IT YOUR WAY—
TO WIN, YOU MUST SURRENDER!

Mark Kastleman

I HAVE OFTEN BEEN ASKED, "Mark, of all the recovery principles and tools, which do you consider to be *the* most important?" For me, the response is immediate, sure and requires but a single word: *grace.* The infinite and enabling power of grace through the Atonement of our Savior Jesus Christ, instantly accessible to you and me in each moment, *is* the heart and soul of our recovery. Grace is *His part.*

If you were to inquire, "Mark, when it comes to *our part,* what is the most critical recovery principle or tool?" Again, my answer would be instant and certain, and also expressed in a single word. It is both a principle and a tool. It is remarkably simple yet deeply profound. It is our natural, eternal way of *being* and at the same time can be excruciatingly difficult to implement. This master principle and tool is called *surrender.*

When I was first introduced to the recovery concept of surrender, my resistance was instant and intense: "Are you recovery people crazy! You can't surrender *and* win at the same time! You don't curl up in the fetal position and wave the cowardly white flag! You stand your ground, put up your fists and fight! You never, ever give in!"

This reaction was proof that I had no understanding of *surrender* from the standpoint of recovery and the teachings of Jesus Christ. It required many years of painful trial and error for me to finally comprehend, accept, embrace and seek to consistently practice surrender from moment to moment in my daily life. *Grace entwined with surrender* was the Divine formula that finally placed me on the path to lasting freedom from sexual addiction.

Addiction is ALL about CONTROL!

Our sexual addiction is really an advanced form of *control*. We have certain expectations about how we believe our relationships, work, church life, health, finances and our overall lives must unfold in order for us to feel successful, happy and content. And we often go to great lengths to avoid or escape pain, trials and *hard* things. When life doesn't go our way, we can feel many different emotions: fear, anger, disappointment, anxiety, depression, resentment, pessimism, jealousy, shame, unworthiness and many more.

Left to itself, the ego-brain responds to these circumstances and feelings by attempting to control people and things and *force* the outcomes we are convinced we *must* have. The more out-of-control it all becomes, the more the brain intensifies its efforts to exercise even more control. This is when the *Ego-Brain Tendencies* release like a tidal wave. But trying to exert control is a massive energy-drain, and sheer willpower is a quickly exhaustible resource. And EBTs nearly always make things worse. It doesn't take long before we're overwhelmed and *maxed out*. This is when the ego-brain pulls out all the stops and implements its ultimate act of control by seeking what it knows from long experience will bring instant escape, relief and soothing—sexual outlets. In essence, the brain is boldly declaring, "I know exactly how to cover up and soothe these problems and feelings; I know what to do; I know what I need right now; I can handle this my way!"

If we're honest, we can see that "my way" (addiction) is in direct competition with and opposition to "God's way" and is really a form of *pride*.

What is *Surrender* and Why is it SO Difficult?

I love the *12 Steps*. I believe God inspired and directed their creation. In my recovery programs, my clients and I have a favorite saying: *It's as easy as 1-2-3*. This refers to the first three steps in the 12 Step Tradition. In a nutshell, Step One is the admission that by myself I am powerless over my addiction and that my life has become unmanageable. Step Two follows with the natural logic that I must therefore come to believe in, trust and rely on a Power that is greater than me. And, Step Three is my decision to turn my will and my life over to that Power which is the love and care of God.

The first three steps capture the essence of surrender. Here's how one of my clients described his journey through these steps:

All my life I used all kinds of tactics to avoid pain and hard things. I wore masks and put on a good front. I was a people pleaser; I took shortcuts; I avoided and escaped by going to my addiction and then kept it hidden to keep up my reputation. I closed off my true emotions because I didn't want to feel them. I easily went into being negative and pessimistic. I was always trying to control people and things so that my life would be easier.

The problem was, the more I tried to control it all and do it my way, the more things fell apart, until my life was in ruins. I found myself going to my addiction more and more often until it dominated my life. It took many, many years of stupid choices and a lot of wreckage, but finally I got to the place where I could admit, "I can't do this anymore! My way is a disaster and I'm hopelessly caught in addiction and I can't break out; I'll never get free. I guess you could say that I finally cried, "Uncle!"

I finally was ready and totally willing to stop doing everything "my way" and start turning my life over to God and doing things "His way." I was finally ready to truly surrender.

Surrender is difficult because the ego-brain doesn't want to give up control. It fears an uncertain and unpredictable future and believes it can actually control outcomes by doing things its way. The thought of surrendering all of that control, giving it over to God and trusting the future entirely to His wisdom and care, is frightening! Equally unnerving is the idea of actually bringing to light all of the ego-brain's tendencies and working to surrender and replace them! But most terrifying of all is the realization within the ego-brain that it might actually have to entirely surrender and give up its powerful and reliable sexual outlets; the place it retreats to for escape and self-soothing when life gets hard. A close friend in recovery shared his fears about surrender:

> It was easy to say I was entirely ready to surrender my addiction and my old behaviors, but when I got really honest it scared the life out of me! How was I going to cope when life got really hard? What if God's solutions were painful and difficult? My brain knew just where to run to whenever I needed my fix. Now I was facing the commitment that I would take that option off the table and put myself entirely in God's hands. I was petrified!

One might ask, "If surrender is so hard and terrifying, why do it?" I recall the first time I allowed my heart and mind to be fully opened to the principle of surrender. It hit me like a lightning bolt! For decades I had tried to do things my way. I had attempted to control people, circumstances and outcomes. In times of great stress, difficulty, pain and trial I had allowed my ego-brain to take me to sexual addiction behaviors as the number one choice for escape and relief. I had been relying on my power, my logic and reasoning, my wisdom—a tiny, limited, finite resource housed in the computer between my ears!

And there all the time was instant and full access to the infinite love, power, wisdom, knowledge and grace of God! All I had to do was stop and willingly surrender my way in favor of His way! A tiny 3.5 pound fallen brain of resources in exchange for an entire universe of power! *That* is *surrender!* And to think that I spent decades trying to "go it alone!"

Are You Ready for Surrender?

Are you ready and willing to fully surrender your addiction outlets— doing things "your ego-brain's way" (no matter how hard life becomes) and place yourself entirely in God's hands and doing things "His way?" Are you willing to shine a bright spotlight on all of your ego-brain's tendencies and begin surrendering them in favor of your Eternal Self attributes? Are you prepared to stop allowing your ego-brain to run the show? Are YOU—enabled by the grace and Spirit of God, yoked with Christ—ready to take your rightful place in the driver's seat of life and move forward?

Let's be real and admit that *surrender* is not a one-time decision. The battle between your fallen ego-brain and your true Eternal Self (to *act* or *be acted upon*) is one you will face every day of your life. Surrender is a daily principle and tool you must practice and perfect until it simply becomes who you are and what you do.

As you progress forward in your recovery, you will find it necessary to surrender and *place on the altar,* all sorts of thoughts, behaviors, tendencies and practices that have been *your way of doing things;* anything that sets you up for or makes you vulnerable to sexual addiction behaviors. This list is unique to each individual, but common items could include: exchanging your smartphone for a flip phone; only accessing the Internet with a partner; installing accountability software on all your devices; canceling your cable TV subscription; taking a different route to work; refusing to allow any type of sexual fantasy or imagining to play on the stage of your mind, (even fantasies about your wife); eliminating movies with *any* sexual content or innuendo; not allowing favorite EBTs to play on your mind's stage like anger, fear, shame, resentment, rationalization, procrastination, pride, laziness, pessimism, negativism, etc.

As you can see, surrender is no trivial matter! It requires you to give up to God anything and everything that is playing a role in you remaining trapped in addiction. Now, please don't be overwhelmed! Surrender is not an *all or nothing* nor an *all at once* proposition. It is a steady, consistent daily journey and process that takes time, patience and dedication. Under the inspiration of Heaven and with the aid of grace, you will choose the most critical things to surrender first, work on those, and progress steadily down your list, one moment and one day at a time.

A Simple Surrender Tool

It can be difficult to understand exactly *how* to surrender in a moment of unwanted thoughts, sexual urges or dominant ego-brain tendencies. Here's a simple surrender tool that has worked extremely well for my clients and me:

1. **Be Aware:** Identify the moment an unwanted thought, urge or tendency enters the stage of your mind.

2. **Pause and Observe:** Don't panic, fight or give in—simply pause, take a few deep breaths and observe.

3. **Surrender it up to God:** Converse with God and say, "Father, I could use my agency to simply go with this thought I'm having; I could let it take over; but instead I am choosing to surrender it to you; here you go." (I actually make a motion with my hands and arms, literally giving it over to God.)

4. **Ask for a Replacement:** Once you surrender it over, you ask God, "Father, I've given that over to you. What do I need most in this moment?" Be quiet, be still and listen/feel for ideas, impressions or insights—they will come. This is you tapping into grace and receiving guidance.

5. **DO IT NOW!** When the idea or insight comes, don't allow your ego-brain to hesitate, rationalize or procrastinate—**Act NOW!** It could be implementing one of several dozen highly effective recovery tools; taking a break to get a bite to eat; calling/texting a friend or family member; listening to uplifting music; doing a simple act of service; writing down your blessings; gazing at a photo of your wife and children; pondering on a favorite scripture; or simply standing up and leaving the room. Whatever it is, **act on it NOW!**

Don't be surprised if you find it necessary to repeat this surrender process multiple times each day for the same relentless thoughts and urges. You have spent years or decades allowing these things to dominate the stage of your mind; they have become *wired* into your subconscious. It will take time and consistent effort and practice to rewire and replace them. But it absolutely will happen—just stick with it!

We all find this surrender process to be new and different. Yet God has counseled us throughout the scriptures to use this very principle and tool:

"Counsel with the Lord in <u>all</u> thy doings." (Alma 37:37)

"Look unto me in every thought; doubt not, fear not." (D&C 6:36)

"The Holy Ghost . . . will show unto you all things what ye should do." (2 Nephi 32:5)

"But behold, I say unto you that ye must pray always, and not faint; that ye must not perform anything unto the Lord save in the first place ye shall pray unto the Father in the name of Christ, that He will consecrate thy performance unto thee, that thy performance may be for the welfare of thy soul." (2 Nephi 32:5)

RECOVERY REQUIRES *REAL* CONNECTION

Mark Kastleman

THE FINAL CHAPTER in Section One makes a bold declaration: *addiction is an intimacy disorder!* As I reflect on my own addiction struggles, and those of the men I've counseled over the years, I know this statement to be accurate. Here are a few insights from that chapter:

> The simplest way I know to understand intimacy in its truest form is through hyphenating the word itself: in-to-me-you-see. True intimacy is manifest in the courageous, vulnerable act of allowing others to see us at our raw and real core, without walls, masks, facades, charades or pretense. In-to-me-you-see with all of my sins, flaws, darkness, weakness and foolishness; and my strengths, innate goodness, beauty, light, righteous desires and amazingness! With true intimacy, what you see is what you get—how liberating!

> True intimacy IS our natural state; we long for it and must have it to feel safe, fulfilled and joyful; to be physically, emotionally and spiritually healthy. Yet we fear that which we most need —"I want to reveal my true, innermost self to you but I'm scared to death that when you find out who I really am you will reject me!" So we seek to fill our natural need for intimacy in ways we perceive to be free of the risks of transparency and vulnerability.

I have already elaborated at length about the two recovery principles/tools I consider to be above all others in power and importance: *grace* (His part) and *surrender* (our part). Nowhere will you find these two in more complete harmony than in the pursuit of true intimacy or *real* connection. Pulling out *all* the stops and allowing others (and yourself) to *see* you as you truly are, in your raw, honest, vulnerable state, is an act of total surrender! And the reason you should be willing take this terrifying risk? Because Jesus has you in the hollow of His strong and loving hands—His *grace* covers you and guarantees that no matter how difficult, no matter how extreme the initial consequences might seem, through Him *all* things work for your good, your learning, your growth and your happiness.

If you are to break free from the iron shackles of sexual compulsion and addiction, you must be ready and willing to surrender your fears, awkwardness, exterior facades, pride, pretending and habit of hiding to learn and practice *real connection*. This is what will fill the intimacy void and hole in your soul—a primary reason you turn to sexual outlets in the first place! This real connection is your eternal way of being; it's what you knew and lived in each moment in your heavenly home.

All on its own, the art of true intimacy and real connection could easily occupy an entire book. What follows are some brief guidelines to start you down the intimacy/connection path.

A Real Connection with God

A combination of religious culture and deep feelings of shame and unworthiness can create a rigidly formal, distant, disconnected and fear-based relationship with God. Your fallen brain can easily conjure up an unapproachable and unreachable Being who is regularly disappointed, often disgusted and, at best, tolerates you.

This is not the unconditionally loving and accepting, infinitely patient, and anxious-to-forgive Heavenly Father revealed by our beloved Savior. In John 14:9, Jesus taught His disciples, *"He that hath seen Me hath seen the Father."* And in John 5:19 He declares, *"The Son can do nothing of himself, but what he seeth the Father do: for what things soever he doeth, these also doeth the Son likewise."*

If you desire to know your Heavenly Father—His attributes, His demeanor, His feelings for you—look no further than the earthly ministry of His Son. Jesus followed the example of His Father in lovingly lifting and healing publicans and sinners; the sick and afflicted; the broken and downtrodden; the hopeless and outcast; and yes, even the addicted.

To succeed in recovery, you must open your heart and mind to a loving and approachable Father who longs to hear from you in honest and vulnerable heart-felt conversation (prayer). You must set aside the conjured shame of the fallen brain and engage in a real heart-to-heart connection and intimacy with your Heavenly Father—*into-me-He-sees*.

In addition, you also need to seek to bind yourself to Christ in every thought and in every moment. One intimacy tool I use is a favorite portrait of Christ. I have it as the background image on my phone. I also carry a 7x9 framed version with me throughout the day so I can continually see His face. It's visible when I shower and shave; it's on my desk while I work; it's in my car while I commute; it's by my bedside while I sleep. This is one of my ways of trying to stay connected to Him and remember Him always. It helps me continually feel the warm and loving embrace of His infinite grace.

Another significant tool in your quest to stay connected to God should be a daily appointment with Him where you talk and ponder on His written words. Your brain seeks routine, structure and habituation. Schedule your intimate, close time with your Heavenly Father and Savior and hold it as your most important appointment. I highly recommend starting and ending your day in this way. And remember, real connection is always two-way communication: have a pad and pen ready to record God's side of the conversation as you open your heart and mind to receive His promptings.

Also look for spontaneous, natural-flow-of-life opportunities to connect with God. Drive time is an excellent chance to have a conversation with Him, listen to His words and enjoy inspirational music. Eating lunch, waiting for a meeting to begin or taking a break to go for a walk are excellent windows of time to connect with God. Get in the habit of anticipating and seeking opportunities to spend time with Him!

A Connection with Self

A real connection with yourself may sound like a bit of a contradiction—"What do you mean connect to myself? I am me!" In an earlier chapter you learned that "you," (your true Eternal Self) are not your brain. You are a dual being consisting of an intelligent, eternal spirit temporarily dwelling within a mortal body. To have a real connection with yourself you must come to realize who you truly are: a literal Eternal Child of God who lived with Him for eons of time! And you must develop the skill of distinguishing between the Eternal You and your fallen body and ego-brain. You must step back and become an observer of your brain's thoughts and emotions, and the sensations and feelings of your body.

I like to think of this as *self-intimacy—into-me-I-see*. Fully focused on survival, the ego-brain goes to great lengths to prevent you from peeling back the layers and shining the bright spotlight on all of "its" tendencies, weaknesses and flaws. It skirts the underlying issues that trigger you into avoiding, escaping and self-medicating through addiction. The brain seeks to keep all of this hidden, covered over and permanently buried. You can learn to do just the opposite and take every opportunity for brutal self-honesty, self-analysis and purposely bring these things into the light where they can be addressed and healed. Here are some basic, highly effective self-intimacy tools that you can integrate into your daily life

- **Daily Personal Inventory:** At the close of each day, take time to stand back and look at all of the Ego-Brain-Tendencies and Eternal Self Attributes that were active in your life over the last 24 hours. Give your EBTs and ESAs a daily score to notice trends, areas for focus, improvements, ruts, etc. This is one of the most effective self-connection tools you will ever use. I highly recommend that you implement it on a daily basis.

- **Daily *Feelings* Journal:** This is not a factual "I-came-I-saw-I-went-I-did" log of your daily life. It's an opportunity for you to let down all of your ego-brain's masks and defenses and simply express your most raw and real feelings and emotions—whatever happens to be dominating the stage of your mind at the time. Don't worry about grammar, structure or language—just let it flow. Ask God in fervent prayer to help you get in touch with these deep issues. And remember, these entries are for your eyes only! Keep them password-protected or under lock and key. If you have a particular entry that is especially negative or caustic and not to be viewed by anyone, then erase or destroy it. The main objective is getting it all out as opposed to keeping it buried, where it festers and eventually leads to acting out.

- **Daily Meditation/Mindfulness:** For years I attempted to engage in the traditional empty-your-mind type of meditation. It left me frustrated and shamed because I could never manage to keep my mind blank for more than ten or twelve seconds! I discovered that directed meditation—with a specific theme or focus—worked much better for me. It was all about shifting from the tiny stage of my mind to the infinite stage of God's mind; accessing a fullness of mind or *mindfulness*. I use my meditation time to simply relax, be still and focus on my Savior. I visualize myself with Him during His ministry. At other times I simply imagine Him embracing, loving and accepting me and I allow that feeling to wash over me. Sometimes I see and feel myself connected to Him, my family and everyone on earth by rays of light, and I immerse myself in that joyous sensation of total oneness. Be creative, the possibilities are endless! You can seek out guided meditations online to get a feel for how it works.

A Real Connection with Others

This is perhaps that most difficult connection of all. The ego-brain tends to continually default toward guarded relationships and controlled interactions where we only permit others a limited view of who we are. We share only what we want them to see, or believe they need to see, in order to approve of and accept us. We put our best foot forward; say the right words; wear the right clothes; project the right image; try to fit in; avoid making waves; put on a show. We do anything we can to avoid being our real, raw, honest, vulnerable and genuine self.

It takes incredible courage and humility to allow ourselves to have a real connection with those around us. There is only one way I know of overriding the ego-brain to achieve this true intimacy: relying on and trusting the empowering and enabling grace of Jesus Christ, and surrendering our Ego-Brain-Tendencies in the moment. We must set aside the masks, pretenses and hiding to let others see the raw and real whole of us with all of our flaws, weaknesses, fears, foibles, talents, gifts, uniqueness, caring, compassion—all of us! This ability and skill does NOT develop in an instant! We have formed these habits of disconnection over a lifetime and we can only evolve and transform them with time, patience and practice.

Realize that there are many forms of human intimacy. These can be broken down into eight categories. Doing so helps us see that we can practice and perfect the art of intimacy in our lives in many small, natural ways that don't seem so daunting. The following list was developed to help us be more holistically intimate with our wives. In each area, we try to immerse ourselves and be fully present in the moment. Many of these can also be used in making real connection with the people that are all around us every day:

1. **Spiritual:** Sharing something of your own sacred feelings and spiritual journey with one another.

2. **Emotional:** Sharing of personal feelings, accompanied by expectations of understanding, affirmation, and demonstration of caring.

3. **Intellectual:** Coming together to share ideas and thoughts, and feeling open and comfortable doing so, even when your opinions differ.

4. **Physical:** Engaging in non-sexual physical activities together through exercise, sports, dancing, outdoor pursuits, hobbies, etc.

5. **Social:** Sharing social activities together, which may include being with groups like family and friends.

6. **Affectional:** Non-sexual contact and interaction that demonstrates and communicates closeness, appreciation and friendship.

7. **Aesthetic:** Sharing something beautiful together such as strolling through a botanical garden, an art museum, listening to a live band or watching a lightning storm.

8. **Sexual:** In partnership with God, come together to express and enjoy the sacred power that co-creates "life"—the life of a marriage relationship celebrated in a literal "oneness" of body, mind, emotion and spirit.

TAKING THE FIGHT TO THE ENEMY

Stephen Moore

IN WARTIME, when both sides are undeviatingly at odds with each other, there can only be one victor. One side wins, the other side loses, and to the victor goes the spoils. The war you are engaged in with your addiction *is just that: a war.* The stakes? Your marriage. Your inner peace. Your relationships. Your soul. Denial is a powerful numbing agent. It acts like an emotional, mental and spiritual pain suppressant, numbing you to the significance of the struggle you are engaged in.

"This has to stop!"

During the war with my addicted self, I have often declared, "This has to stop!" At first, it was usually after a long binge in my addiction and was typically preceded by a significant consequence: almost losing a job for looking at pornography at work; being caught while acting out in some fashion; losing my temper and saying things I immediately regretted to loved ones. I have whispered, "This has to stop!" to myself half-heartedly in my mind, even as I was planning my next relapse. I have screamed it at God, in anger for His apparent unwillingness to heal me (a distorted view at the time, but reality for me), and out of hatred over my inability to say "no" to my addiction. I have sobbed it through desperate tears of shame and regret, pleading for deliverance from God, even though I believed He had abandoned me due to my mounting history of failure.

Later in the process, I began to say, "This has to stop!" with a little more determination and resolve; perhaps after a relapse following an increased period of sobriety. Soon, I was speaking it to myself as I worked through the 12 Steps and came to understand the significance of my poor choices. Now, I often find myself saying it following counseling sessions as I work with men and women in the trenches, struggling to find respite from their own frailties and poor choices. I find myself saying it after nearly every meeting with a traumatized wife who is desperate to save her marriage, but racked with shame, sadness and anger. I have whispered it to myself many times while co-authoring this book, and I am going to say it one more time, to you, the reader: "This has to stop!"

When I work with clients, I often discuss adopting a "war mentality" in recovery. If there is one truth that I have learned in the fight against addiction, it is this: *it is you or him.* This means that it's your Soul or Your Addiction: you can't have both. Oil or Water. Peace or Strife. Connection or Isolation. None of these things are compatible with its opposite. *The time for fence-sitting is over.* In the long run, either you or your addiction will emerge victorious. Now is the time to take the fight to the enemy. You don't have to be perfect in your recovery journey, but you have to remain committed. There is no turning back. It's time to slay the dragon.

Hold the Line

In the war of recovery, just as in a physical war, some days will be harder than others. In measuring your progress, focus on the direction you're moving while accounting for what you are up against emotionally and spiritually. Victory has many different faces.

I once had a client who was struggling to find lasting sobriety. Like many of us, he was struggling to hold himself accountable. He came into my office, head down, unable to make eye contact and slumped onto my couch with a loud sigh. Anticipating a discussion about what was beginning to look like a recent relapse, I asked him how he was doing. "Miserable! I'm a failure!" was the reply. I asked him to elaborate; he told me how he had been tempted to act out sexually in various forms all week. He had been diligently using his tools to remain sober, but would find respite for only a short time before the next wave of temptation would wash over him. He told me that he had not relapsed, but felt hopeless because a part of him still desired to do so.

We had a discussion about measuring victory in the war of recovery. Sometimes in war, to be victorious means to *hold the line*—to be attacked by the enemy again and again so it seems you are doing little more than holding the line. Progress seems nonexistent; it's all you can do to not act out. *Don't mistake such days as defeat.* Again, success in recovery takes many different forms. A day where you live to fight again tomorrow with minimal casualties is significant progress.

Taking Back Ground

I have a phrase that I use often in my work with clients: *you should be challenged every day in recovery.* If this isn't the case, you are likely not working hard enough on your recovery program. Specifically, you should be pushed in one of two ways on a daily basis: either your addiction is pressing the attack on you (like my example above), or you are working to take back enemy territory. This means expanding your recovery work and knowledge, and establishing connections with yourself and with others.

The key to recovery isn't merely to defend yourself, even though it's tempting to "take a break" from recovery during times when simply being sober seems like a victory. More often than not, this is a mistake. Apathy and getting comfortable in the recovery process are some of your greatest enemies. If real change is going to take place, your efforts must be consistent. Days where your addiction is exerting less of a pull on you should not be seen as a chance to rest on your laurels. These are days when you can expand your understanding of your addiction; cultivate mindfulness; journal and develop new recovery strategies for bad days; and work on the trauma and shame underlying your addiction.

Always Prepared to Do Battle

It's critical to always be prepared for battle. Particularly in the early stages of recovery, an addict's mental state can appear to shift almost instantly. Something stressful occurs at work; your spouse is struggling with her own feelings or issues; you feel underappreciated by someone; your coworker wears a low-cut shirt. A variety of environments and emotions can take you quickly to a place where acting out goes from being a silly idea to a very real possibility. In moments like these, what largely determines victory or defeat is what you have done to prepare beforehand. *What have your recovery efforts been like today? Yesterday? The past week?* What you were doing for recovery during those times often determines your fate today. In the next chapter, we will discuss the practical realities of preparation for the fight of your life: your battle for inner peace and personal freedom from addiction and shame.

CREATING YOUR BATTLE PLAN FOR SUCCESSFUL RECOVERY

Stephen Moore

"How are you feeling?" I asked Brett through the wall as we were both changing clothes. "Amazing; I'm nervous but excited," was the reply. He asked me the same question. "This is about as good as it gets for me," I said. Having finished changing, we both stepped out of our stalls, dressed in white clothing. Alone in the room just outside the baptismal font, we embraced, and I will never forget the look of joy and excitement in Brett's eyes. After the baptism, I saw a greater measure of something he had been lacking for much of his life: a sense of peace. I was privileged to witness first-hand the power that recovery has in changing a man's whole world.

A lot of preparation had gone into that day: the bishop arrived a few hours prior to fill the baptismal font; family and friends had changed schedules to be there for the occasion. People had given up time on their weekend to show up at a small chapel for what some might consider a common event. After all, baptisms in the LDS Church are a regular occurrence in Utah. But for Brett, his wife and family members, that day was anything but routine.

Re-baptism marked the culmination of a journey that Brett had been on for much of his life. He spent years struggling to break the chains of sexual addiction. His attempts at recovery had usually consisted of small but temporary fixes; sincere but ineffective attempts at finding lasting change. If I could somehow introduce the man in white to the person Brett had been on the day of our first counseling session, I don't know if they would recognize each other.

In our first meeting, Brett told me he wasn't even sure if he wanted recovery; he wasn't sure if his marriage was salvageable. He struggled to see how there was any hope for the future. He felt broken, beaten down and depressed. He was angry with himself and resented the people closest to him. Many times while writing this book, I have thought about Brett and many other clients; I have thought about myself; and I have thought a great deal about you, the reader. Many of you can relate to Brett, as I can. If anyone had told Brett during that first counseling session about the changes he would make in future months and years, he would not have believed it.

I will share with you the highlights of some things I shared with Brett that first day on how we would work together to lay a solid foundation for his recovery journey; what recovery looks like in the trenches; and a description of the day-to-day fight with his dark side. That path to recovery worked for him. It worked for me. And I guarantee it can work for you. As authors, we challenge you to start this journey with sincerity and fully apply yourself so you can experience the significant changes that await. The road to recovery is long and has many twists and turns. Here is where it begins: the first day of the rest of your life.

1. Envision the Recovery You Want and Commit to It

To successfully make this journey, you must know where you want to go. Paint a picture in your mind, then *write it down and be detailed about it.* Envision your family: what do you want it to look like a month from now? A year from now? Five years from now? Is everyone smiling and genuinely happy, or are the smiles forced, the feelings of love for each other poisoned with the chaos of addiction? When you look at your wife or imagine your future bride, what do you want to see in her eyes? Trust and adoration? Or pain, sorrow and fear? Once you have done the writing, hang it up somewhere or put a copy in your wallet; add to or change it as your vision grows. Doing this provides you with a solid foothold going forward. So here we go; what follows is your roadmap to recovery.

2. Connect With Other Addicts in Recovery

Recovery without accountability is impossible. As we have discussed in previous chapters, your support system is key. Find a sponsor and commit to contacting him at least daily. Find and attend some kind of recovery meetings with a therapist or a 12-Step group. Shop around; attend several different meetings. Commit to one, and make it your "home group"—the group you attend each week. There is no adequate substitute for these meetings. I rarely miss my Sexaholics Anonymous group meetings, and consider them fundamental to my spirituality and recovery. Surround yourself with support people and commit to contacting more than one of them each day about how you are *really* doing. *You should begin by making either phone-based or in-person contact with someone in recovery each morning and evening, and begin attending at least one 12-Step recovery group or therapist-led group each week.*

3. Get Honest With Those You Need To

Early in the process, most of us continue to keep secrets: from ourselves and others. Who do you need to get honest with about the depth and reality of your addiction? Is it a bishop? A spouse? Yourself? Without honesty in recovery, you will have very little success. *Begin this process as soon as possible. Commit to getting honest with at least one person each week, and don't stop attempting these conversations until you are successful with being accountable to someone. Also, commit to five minutes of daily journaling about your progress; practice recognizing and expressing feelings.*

4. Collaborate With God

Start where you are. Take at least one step to further develop a spiritual relationship with God every day. Be creative about it. Learn about who God is to you, and work with others to identify any flaws in your thinking as you start allowing Him into your life. Most of us have a very distorted view of God at the start; I did, and I was raised in the church my entire life. Look for ways that God can become your ally in this battle. It may sound simple, but many of us struggle with this. Talk to Him. Ask Him to guide you. Be bold and courageous. Fight through your shame, and trust that you are a son of God, and that no matter what you have done, you are not beyond rescue. *Begin by doing this for five minutes each morning. Prayer, spiritual study, meditation, or uninterrupted quiet time is a good start.*

5. Develop Your Own Kit of Recovery Tools

The tools provide in this book are a collection of exercises, activities, resources and practices that help build you emotionally and spiritually in the recovery process. There are many others we can't include for the sake of space. You pick up these tools over time: counselors, 12-Step meetings, sponsors, trial and error, and inspiration are all good sources. As you develop this bag of "tools," keep in mind that the goal isn't to use every tool every day. Rather, choose several and incorporate them into your recovery journey that day.

As you select them, choose *at least one that you want to do the least*. There's a reason you feel an aversion to it, and those activities you're resisting can help you gain the most ground in your recovery journey. I can promise you that not only will this become more enjoyable over time, it's also the best thing you can do for yourself, your family, and anyone or anything else that is precious to you. Remember, *good recovery involves learning to be selfish in healthy ways*. Put yourself first in the right ways, and the rest has a way of falling into place. *I strongly recommend a blend of three to five activities (including the ones in this chapter) over the course of at least 30 minutes each day. You should add to this effort as often as possible, and rotate them regularly.*

6. Daily Step Work and Study

You will learn more about this as you begin attending meetings, get a sponsor or begin working with a therapist, but the most successful path that works consistently in a good daily recovery routine is to *work on progressing through the 12 Steps.* I have yet to see lasting recovery for anyone who doesn't involve daily Step-work in their routine. *You should begin with studying the 12 Steps, and rapidly implement them. Do this at least 10 minutes a day.*

7. Find a Professional

Finding a counselor or therapist that can help you build a strong spiritual foundation is critical to your recovery. Many professionals shy away from discussing spiritual topics; we encourage you to find someone willing to explore this openly in a way that helps you connect more deeply with God. In addition to encouraging your spirituality, you need a professional who can help you address your thinking errors, character liabilities and other addiction issues. I've been sober for years, but continue to see a therapist regularly. Your recovery journey will be faster and more effective, and your relationships will have a better chance of surviving and thriving. *Do this as soon as possible, and commit to weekly therapy at first.*

Believe In Yourself. Trust Us. You Can Do This.

When Brett and I went back to the locker room following his re-baptism—signaling a commitment to his recovery and his covenants—I asked him the same question I had asked before: "Well, how do you feel?" He paused, looked at me with a peace in his eyes, and simply answered, "*different.*"

My friend, envision milestones like this in your own recovery journey; the ones that await you as you progress in this most sacred of battles. In what ways do you want to both feel and be "different?" In what ways is your wife hoping and praying for you to be "different?" Your children? Your Maker?

Above all, please remember: don't give up. The journey to recovery is often a long one. Your failures of the past, however many and significant they may be, don't dictate your future. There is such a thing as a last relapse. Your goal is not to be "cured" tomorrow; your goal is to be a little better today than you were yesterday. It is a one-day-at-a-time journey. May you look back on today as one of those times where you drew a line in the sand with your addiction, and resolved to move forward on the road to connection, happiness and peace.

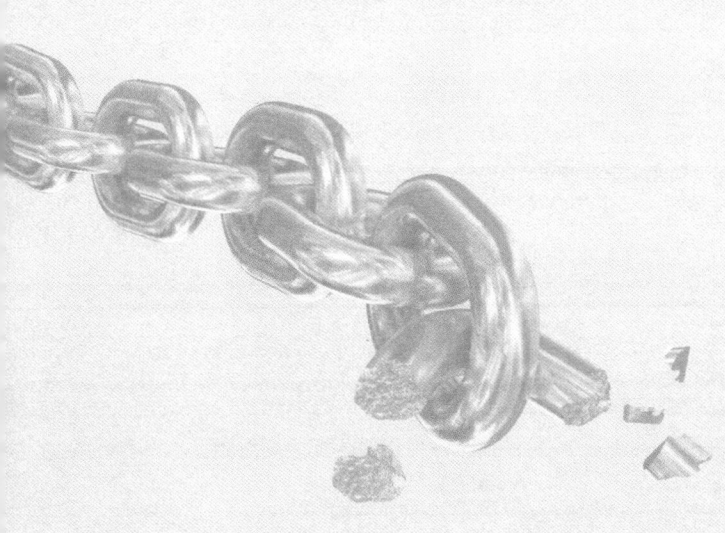

ADDITIONAL HELP

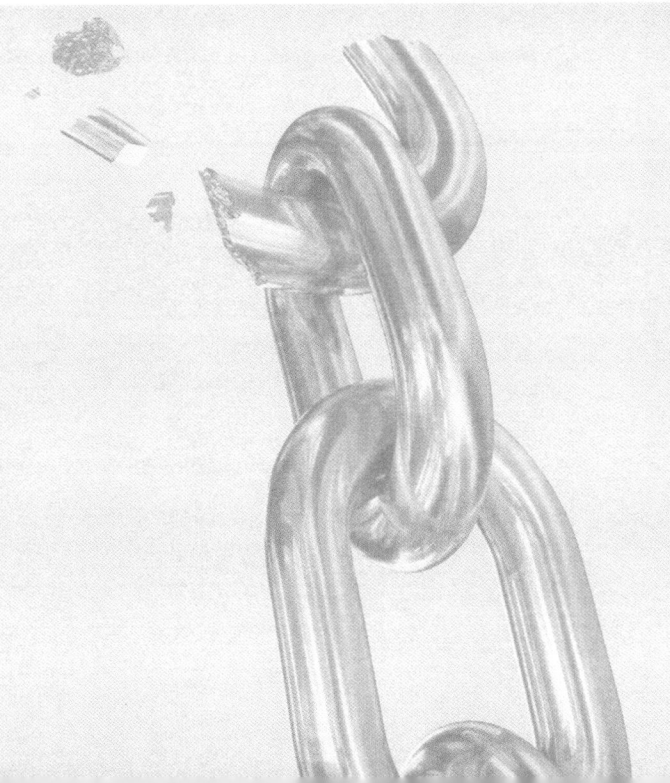

FOR THE SPOUSE OF AN ADDICT

Every time we meet with spouses of sexual addicts, grappling with the trauma of a husband's betrayal, our hearts go out to them. In the faces of these amazing women, we see echoes of our own wives, and the anguish that our poor choices have caused; the tears we've been responsible for; the sadness we've brought them. And it isn't fair.

This is not a trial you asked for. No woman enters a marriage expecting to deal with a situation of this magnitude. No wife kneels at an altar in the temple dreaming that such poison is on the horizon. Perhaps you were aware of your husband's addiction before marriage, but were unaware of how serious it was. Perhaps your husband concealed or downplayed his past prior to marriage, or his addictive tendencies didn't start until after you were married. It doesn't really matter, because no matter the circumstance, it isn't fair. You did nothing to deserve this. And it's not your fault.

If you find yourself grappling with these issues, please believe us when we say *you are not responsible for your husband's addiction*. There is so much more we want to say about this (and we will, in our next book), but for now, please practice trusting in the fact that it is *not* your fault. Your husband and others may blame you, either inferring or claiming outright that a better sexual relationship with you, for example, could have or would have prevented his addiction. This is absolutely false. Though it may be difficult to accept (particularly for the addict), the faster you and your spouse can agree on the fact that his addiction is his responsibility, the faster you will make real progress in the recovery process. Are there actions you can take that would improve your marriage? Probably. But that doesn't mean you are in any way responsible for his betrayal! True accountability is the bedrock of healing.

Love Your Marriage Enough to Focus On You

For many of the women we work with, discovering their husband's addiction propels them to hyper vigilance over their spouse's recovery: they often become the policewoman in the marriage; the absolver of their husband's indiscretions; the keeper of their husband's secrets. The line between love and enablement in the recovery process is a thin one; often the actions a spouse takes from a place of love actually enable further inappropriate behavior. Often, a spouse will try to work on the marriage itself, or work to compensate in various ways for her husband's seemingly greater-than-normal need for sex. There is no body type, sexual position, set of lingerie or physical enhancement that would have prevented your husband's addiction. Sadly, trying to compensate in these ways (again from a place of wanting to help the marriage) can actually cause further damage, both to you through self-betrayal and through feeding your husband's use of sex as a way of coping and escaping from life's challenges.

The best way you can work on your marriage may actually seem counterintuitive: it is to focus on yourself and your own healing first. Doing so will give your marriage a chance to really succeed. To be clear, we aren't saying that you shouldn't support your husband and his recovery; nothing can be further from the truth. But learning to do so in healthy ways without compromising your own values, standards or expectations for fidelity is the key.

It Begins with Boundaries: Loving Yourself

Healthy recovery from betrayal trauma for a spouse begins with learning what your needs are, both inside and outside of your marriage relationship, and then working to establish healthy boundaries around those needs. Your emotional safety needs to be protected at all costs.

There is often resistance from a husband when this process begins. For example, a wife who doesn't feel emotionally safe to connect sexually with her spouse may experience pressure, either from her spouse, family members or other misinformed parties, to do so before she is ready. These people are wrong. Marriage covenants between a husband and wife, including eternal covenants, do not require one partner to compromise who they are for the sake of either their spouse or the relationship. If you find yourself in this position, the guidance of a good therapist can be very helpful. A skilled professional can help teach you how to set healthy boundaries both for yourself and your relationship.

Setting these boundaries requires real change, but believe us when we say, "It's worth it!" When each of our wives began taking such actions early in our recovery process, we mistakenly resisted in some ways. Even as professionals, we were afraid of change and losing our marriages. But when our wives loved us enough to hold boundaries with us and within the marriage, though frustrating and difficult, their determination was vital for our recovery and the stability of our marriages. It allowed us to learn to hold ourselves accountable and break through denial. It empowered us to make lasting changes by doing the hard work of recovery. We thank God every day for the courage and bravery our wives displayed in those moments when they loved us enough to stand up to our addiction-based thinking and actions.

There is Hope!

Things may look bleak for you at this moment; you likely have much fear and anxiety for the future. Stay the course. Good recovery for you involves learning to put yourself first in healthy ways. The beauty of your individual recovery process is that it doesn't require your husband to recover along with you. Though you probably would like nothing more than to see him recover alongside you, we promise you can get better whether he chooses to take that step with you or not. You can grow, overcome, and regain (or in some cases, find for the first time) your confidence and self-worth. Your recovery and growth is your own, no matter who you live with.

We are living proof that marriages, however broken, have the ability to heal if both partners are truly committed and willing to do what is necessary. Beyond the darkest lows in your marriage there lies the potential for the greatest highs. Investing in yourself is the best thing you can do for your marriage. Find a good counselor or therapist. Expand your support system. Surround yourself with friends and others who understand. You are enough just as you are. You are valued. You are worth it.

CAN OUR MARRIAGE SURVIVE?

Imagine for a moment what life was like in your heavenly home, through the eons of time before and leading up to this mortal experience. Did you have close, cherished relationships? Were you acquainted with your future husband or wife in the world before this one? (The words of scripture and the prophets echo a resounding "Yes!") How did you *see* one another in relation to your eternal potential and your infinite intrinsic worth, your hopes and dreams for mortality and the eternities beyond?

You may be wondering, "What does all of this have to do with my marriage here and now?" Our response is, "Everything!"

Every couple that successfully travels the very difficult and sometimes treacherous path of recovery and healing, questions how they can possibly make it through. The journey is a rollercoaster ride of ups and downs, successes and failures, great joys and deep sorrows, triumphs and tragedies. Hovering over all of it is the intensifying influence of addiction and betrayal trauma. There are times when the burdens exceed a couple's capacity to bear them; when they are tempted to throw in the towel, call it quits and go their separate ways.

If you have doubts and fears about the future of your marriage, you are not alone. Successfully navigating what can at times be a *marital minefield* is a challenge for any couple. But add to that landscape the explosive devastation of sexual addiction, and the challenge is magnified to a whole new level.

There is Great Hope!

As frightening and hopeless as this journey might seem at times, take assurance in the success of others who have been where you are now.

There is great hope for *all* couples, no matter how severe or long-lasting the addiction or broken the relationship. There is a path to healing, forgiveness, reconciliation and lasting happiness together. It will not be easy; in fact, it may be the hardest thing you will ever do together. The reality is, many have done it and so can you. The question is: How?

This *how* is the topic for an entire book (which the authors plan to write soon) but within the limited space of a few pages, here's a brief overview of some bedrock principles. They provide the foundation to rebuild, unify and fortify your marriage, while simultaneously working on recovery and freedom from sexual addiction, and healing betrayal trauma. Take time as a couple to ponder and openly discuss these powerful principles:

1. **Place Christ at the Center of Your Marriage:** Individually and as a couple, you cannot successfully navigate the path of recovery and healing without a LOT of help. The journey is intense, difficult and at times completely overwhelming. The most important, overarching and undergirding source of your power, strength, guidance and support flows from the grace of your Lord and Savior, Jesus Christ. You must literally *yoke* yourselves to Him and place Him at the center of your marriage. You must constantly rely and call upon His grace. He will enable and empower you as a husband to persistently pursue and succeed in your recovery. His grace and tender compassion will enhance and strengthen your natural capacity as a wife to keep loving, forgiving and supporting your husband, even in the midst of your own very real and legitimate feelings of pain, fear, anger, betrayal and fatigue. He will lovingly help you move through these difficult emotions and gently bring you to a place of healing.

2. **Be Willing to Travel Your Own Individual Paths of Healing:** As a husband suffering from sexual addiction you must be ready and willing to do the consistent, daily hard work of recovery in order for your marriage to have any chance of success. You will stumble along the way, but you must never abandon the path and keep pressing forward in recovery for as long as it takes, no matter what! At the same time, it's vital that as a wife, you also receive the support and healing you need. Centered on Christ, enabled and empowered by His grace, you will each travel your own individual paths of healing, giving your marriage the greatest chance to not only survive, but to thrive.

3. **See Each Other with *Eternal Glasses*:** As a woman and wife, because your husband has betrayed you through his sexual addiction behaviors, it is natural and understandable for you to *see* him through the filter of some very valid and intensely negative feelings. This filter can be a significant barrier to you actively supporting him in his recovery. An application of grace that you can call upon to remove this barrier is asking Christ to give you the gift of *seeing* your husband through His eyes; to look beyond the addict behaviors to his *eternal soul*—who he was before this life and who he can become in the eternities ahead. As a husband, you can also petition Christ to help you see your beloved companion through eternal glasses. This approach will aid you both in looking through the façade of this mortal flesh and seeing each other for who you truly are. This will help you find the faith, hope and charity needed for the really tough times.

4. **These Things Shall Give Thee Experience:** You have likely marveled and deeply reverenced the terrible trials and afflictions endured by the prophet Joseph Smith and his remarkable, beloved wife, Emma. In their darkest hours the Lord instructed Joseph, "All these things shall give thee experience, and shall be for thy good." In your current turmoil, this may be a hard pill to swallow. How can the hell of sexual addiction possibly *be for*

your good? If you will cling to Christ and each other, and engage in the hard work and sacrifice of recovery and healing, you will emerge from that crucible experience welded together with a mighty bond that cannot be severed! Truly, God can find a way to transform all of it *for your good.* Of course there are circumstances where a marriage does not survive, yet even then God can turn it all into valuable experience.

5. **Seek Outside Help:** Too often when it comes to navigating the labyrinth of sexual addiction, couples may attempt to *go it alone.* There is no valid reason to bear this impossible burden. Explore and take full advantage of the many readily available resources. These include: working with your bishop and stake president; attending LDS or Sexaholics Anonymous (SA) 12-Step support groups; seeking help from professionals who specialize in sexual addiction, betrayal trauma and counseling with individuals and couples.

HELP FOR PRIESTHOOD LEADERS

WE HAVE A VERY SPECIAL PLACE in our hearts for all of the dedicated bishops and stake presidents throughout the church who selflessly love and lift so many and do so with such mighty faith. We have served with many of these good and remarkable men over the years, and have been served by them in our personal addiction struggles.

After much pondering, prayer and discussion, we believe the most valuable input we can offer to bishops and stake presidents is an inside view of the needs of LDS men who struggle under the heavy burden of sexual addiction. Based on our own personal addiction and recovery experiences, as well as our work with a wide variety of LDS men, here are a few key insights that may help you understand the concerns of a Latter-day Saint experiencing sexual addiction.

1. **I fear disclosure more than I fear death:** I deeply respect you and want you to think well of me and see me as a good man. I fear that if I disclose the true width and depth of my addiction, you will be disappointed, disgusted and never see me the same again. So, I go to great lengths to hide, mask, minimize and understate the severity of my addiction. I may even lie, deflect and deceive. Out of the same feelings of fear and shame, I have also likely hidden my unwanted behaviors from my wife and family. I need you to seek the gift of discernment and see through my facade with compassion, understanding and firmness. Please continue to speak openly about this addiction, and

lovingly invite me to come forward and seek your help. I need you to keep patiently pursuing me for these conversations.

2. **I am outside Christ's Circle:** I have tried countless times to fight and overcome this addiction, and countless times I have failed. I am convinced that my disgusting and despicable behaviors have disqualified me from having access to the help and healing of Christ's Atonement. I believe He is completely disappointed in me and my relentless disobedience; I am outside His circle. I need you to help me truly believe and receive His love and grace. Please also know that harsh, condemning or shaming sermons are not helpful and tend to drive me more deeply into addiction, secrecy and isolation. I already inflict upon myself a sizeable daily dose of shame, unworthiness, self-loathing and self-flogging. I need a true hope-in-Christ that there may actually be a way out for "someone like me."

3. **I am suffering from a *chemical* dependency:** I need you to realize that my sexual addiction is NOT about sex, any more than alcoholism is about the liquid in the glass. I turn to the brain chemical rush of sexual outlets (my drug of choice) to escape, avoid and sooth the uncomfortable, difficult and painful parts of my life. As an integral part of helping me turn from my sexual sins, please also guide me to the help and healing I need for the true underlying issues and deep causes of my behaviors.

4. **I may need more than generalized or traditional help:** Depending on the length of time and severity of my addiction, I may need more help than a traditional 12-Step program or general counseling can provide. When necessary, please encourage me to seek focused help with certified professionals who specialize in sexual addiction and its underlying core issues and causes.

5. **Remember my spouse in all of this:** If I'm married, please realize that my sexual addiction behaviors have caused serious *betrayal trauma-related* symptoms and issues for my wife. She will need to receive qualified help for her own healing journey.

My recovery has the best chance when we are both healthy. And *please* don't be convinced by the argument I may offer that more frequent sexual relations with my wife will cure my *chemical* dependency and heal my deep emotional and spiritual issues. This track will only deepen my addiction, increase my wife's betrayal trauma and create an ever-widening chasm of enmity in our relationship.

We are part of a Team Effort

Bishops and stake presidents, please know that we consider ourselves to be part of a *team* effort. While providing the specialized therapy and counseling needed, we also do all we can to support you in your sacred roles as Judges in Israel. We realize that you are spiritual guides; God's servants who hold the keys of repentance for the men suffering with sexual addiction in your wards and stakes. We not only practice highly effective psychology and proven recovery methods, but also adhere to a strong spiritual approach centered upon Christ and His Atonement.

As a part of our commitment to support bishops and stake presidents, as our schedules permit, we also make ourselves available as presenters on 5th Sundays and at ward and stake firesides. You may contact us through our website at: **www.innerlightsolutionsllc.com**.

CONTACT THE AUTHORS

Stephen Moore, LCSW, CSAT, and Mark Kastleman, BCC, BCPC, specialize in the field of sexual addiction recovery and offer a variety of services, including:

- Individual therapy for men and women
- Couple's therapy
- Group therapy for men and women
- Podcasts, articles and other online resources
- Special recovery and healing retreats for men, women and couples
- Availability to speak on 5th Sundays, at ward and stake firesides, and other events

To learn more about the authors and their services, please visit their website at: www.innerlightsolutionsllc.com

ADDITIONAL RESOURCES

12-Step Support Groups for Addicts
LDS Addiction Recovery Program: www.addictionrecovery.lds.org
Sexaholics Anonymous: www.sa.org

12-Step Support Groups for Spouses and Family members
LDS Addiction Recovery Program: www.addictionrecovery.lds.org
S-Anon: www.sanon.org

ABOUT THE AUTHORS

STEPHEN MOORE is a Licensed Clinical Social Worker who has a strong background in addiction-related treatment and program development, having overseen intensive outpatient programs in the fields of both chemical and sexual addiction for the past 10 years.

Stephen's experience with the individual, familial and societal implications of sex and pornography addiction make him passionate about the need for education and intervention. Stephen has presented to various audiences and appeared in local media discussing the treatment of sexual addiction, the effects of addiction on intimate relationships, and the journey of recovery.

As a Certified Sex Addiction Therapist (CSAT), and as a sex addict in successful recovery himself, Stephen provides a unique treatment methodology. His intimate knowledge of the "addict's world," coupled with extensive specialized training, provides a fresh approach and down-to-earth assistance for those struggling with addiction and their spouses. He owns Ascension Counseling in American Fork, Utah, a private practice focusing exclusively on sex addiction-related issues and betrayal trauma recovery for individuals and couples. (www.ascensioncounselingutah.com)

MARK KASTLEMAN is a Board Certified Clinical Chaplain and Pastoral Counselor with a specialty in addiction recovery and behavior change. For the last 18 years, Mark has focused on providing hope and a path to healing for: men battling with pornography and sexual addiction; wives who bear the heavy burden of betrayal trauma; and couples striving to save their marriages. Mark's intensive, compassionate counseling program *Reclaim* is located in Sandy, Utah. (www.reclaimyourtrueself.com)

In successful long-term recovery from his own struggles with sexual addiction, Mark has a deep empathy and understanding for his clients. After more than 30 years of marriage, Mark and his wife, Ladawn, know the personal heartache and fallout of addiction and what it takes for both spouses to heal and successfully move forward together.

Mark's bestseller, *The Drug of the New Millennium—The Brain Science Behind Internet Pornography Use,* has been published in four languages and is widely cited and utilized by therapists, counselors and clergy.

In 2007, Mark and his team of neuroscientists and psychologists created the online recovery education and support service—*Candéo behaviorchange.com.* Through Candéo, Mark has enjoyed the privilege of teaching and mentoring over 15,000 individuals in more than 80 countries in their struggles with pornography and sexual addiction. As a professional speaker and trainer, Mark has presented to higher education institutions, government agencies, medical and mental health professionals and religious organizations across the U.S. and in many parts of the world.